Paternity Establishment:
Child Support and Beyond

PATERNITY ESTABLISHMENT: CHILD SUPPORT AND BEYOND

CARMEN SOLOMON-FEARS

Novinka Books
New York

Senior Editors: Susan Boriotti and Donna Dennis
Coordinating Editor: Tatiana Shohov
Office Manager: Annette Hellinger
Graphics: Wanda Serrano
Editorial Production: Vladimir Klestov, Matthew Kozlowski and Maya Columbus
Circulation: Ave Maria Gonzalez, Vera Popovic, Luis Aviles, Raymond Davis,
    Melissa Diaz and Jeannie Pappas
Communications and Acquisitions: Serge P. Shohov
Marketing: Cathy DeGregory

Library of Congress Cataloging-in-Publication Data
Available Upon Request

ISBN: 1-59033-510-4.

Copyright © 2003 by Novinka Books, An Imprint of
    Nova Science Publishers, Inc.
    400 Oser Ave, Suite 1600
    Hauppauge, New York 11788-3619
    Tele. 631-231-7269   Fax 631-231-8175
    e-mail: Novascience@earthlink.net
    Web Site: http://www.novapublishers.com

All rights reserved. No part of this book may be reproduced, stored in a retrieval system or transmitted in any form or by any means: electronic, electrostatic, magnetic, tape, mechanical photocopying, recording or otherwise without permission from the publishers.

The authors and publisher have taken care in preparation of this book, but make no expressed or implied warranty of any kind and assume no responsibility for any errors or omissions. No liability is assumed for incidental or consequential damages in connection with or arising out of information contained in this book.

This publication is designed to provide accurate and authoritative information with regard to the subject matter covered herein. It is sold with the clear understanding that the publisher is not engaged in rendering legal or any other professional services. If legal or any other expert assistance is required, the services of a competent person should be sought. FROM A DECLARATION OF PARTICIPANTS JOINTLY ADOPTED BY A COMMITTEE OF THE AMERICAN BAR ASSOCIATION AND A COMMITTEE OF PUBLISHERS.

Printed in the United States of America

CONTENTS

Preface		vii
Introduction		ix
Chapter 1	**Overview**	1
Chapter 2	**Paternity Establishment Process**	7
	Presumptive Paternity for Married Couples	8
	Voluntary Paternity Acknowledgment	9
	Contested Paternity	11
	Genetic Tests	12
Chapter 3	**Paternity Provisions in the CSE Program**	17
	Paternity Establishment Requirements	18
Chapter 4	**Paternity/Fatherhood Provisions in the TANF Program**	25
	Cooperation Requirements	26
	Fatherhood Initiatives	27
	TANF Marriage and Two-Parent Family Goals	28
Chapter 5	**Policy Options to Increase the Level of Paternity Establishment**	31
	Cooperation between Parents and CSE Agencies	32
	Fatherhood Grant Programs	34
	In-Hospital Paternity Establishment	34
	Identifying the Fathers of Older Children	37
Chapter 6	**Other Paternity Issues**	39
	Paternity of Marital Children	39
	Fathers' Rights and Concerns	40
	Mothers' Rights and Concerns	44

Best Interests of the Child	45
Concluding Remarks	46

Appendix A: Legislative History of Paternity
Establishment Provisions — **49**

P.L. 90-248, the Social Security Amendments of 1967	49
P.L. 93-647, the Social Security Amendments of 1974	49
P.L. 94-88, Tariff Amendments, Amendments to Social Security Act-1975	50
P.L. 98-378, the Child Support Enforcement Amendments of 1984	50
P.L 100-485, the Family Support Act of 1988	51
P.L. 103-66, the Omnibus Budget Reconciliation Act of 1993	52
P.L. 104-193, the Personal Responsibility and Work Opportunity Reconciliation Act of 1996	53
P.L. 105-33, The Balanced Budget Act of 1997	54

Index — **55**

PREFACE

Recent years have seen a dramatic increase in children born out of wedlock. Such a situation is of great concern because the poorest demographic group in America is children in single-parent families, which puts great strain on the welfare rolls and adversely impacts the economy. And one should not neglect the influence on the children, who often go through life without a father. Everyone who fathers a child is obligated to at least contribute financially to child support, rather than dodge that responsibility. Consequently, the government has increased its efforts in child support enforcement by establishing paternities through DNA tests and attempting, with the aid of state and local agencies, to apprehend so-called "dead-beat dads."

This book presents background information on paternity establishment and its process, while describing several relevant federal programs and policy options. Included are analyses of genetic testing and the legislative history of this issue. With the increase in single-parent families and the problems they face, the topic of paternity establishment holds great importance to today's society, and this book is a valuable tool in understanding the facts around the issue.

INTRODUCTION

The public policy interest in paternity establishment is based in part on the dramatic increase in nonmarital births. The poorest demographic group in the United States consists of children in single-parent families. In 2000, 33.1% of all U.S. births were to unmarried women, compared to 3.9% in 1950. Moreover, in FY2000, 51.9% of the children in the Child Support Enforcement (CSE) caseload (which includes Temporary Assistance to Needy Families (TANF) and certain other welfare families and non-welfare families who apply for CSE services) were born outside of marriage. The percentage of CSE children who were born outside of marriage varied by state, ranging from 7.8% in Kansas (4% in Puerto Rico) to 79.8% in Delaware.

The main goals of the CSE program are to reduce spending on actual and potential recipients of public welfare by obtaining ongoing support from noncustodial parents; and to establish paternity for children born outside of marriage so that child support can be obtained. Most experts now agree that use of highly reliable DNA tests greatly increases the likelihood of correct identification of putative fathers. DNA tests can be used either to exclude unlikely fathers or to establish a high likelihood that a given man is the father.

With more paternities being established each year than children being born outside of marriage, progress is being made in reducing the number of children who do not have legally established fathers. Nonetheless, Office of Child Support Enforcement (OCSE) data indicate that in FY2000, paternity had been established or acknowledged for only about 65% of the 10.1 million children on the CSE caseload who were born outside of marriage. Some proposals or programs that may increase the numbers of paternities established include: voluntary acknowledgment of paternity especially via hospital-based programs (which increased 781%, from 78,129 in FY1994 to 688,510 in FY2000); a renewed emphasis on older children perhaps through media campaigns; continued outreach to fathers acknowledging their importance to their children; and more cooperation between parents and the CSE agencies. Although many paternity concerns are intermingled with the effectiveness of the CSE program, some are beyond the scope of the CSE program.

This book provides background information on paternity establishment, gives a detailed analysis of the paternity establishment process, describes federal CSE and TANF provisions related to paternity establishment, discusses some policy options to increase the numbers of paternities established, and examines some of the issues related to the establishment of paternity. Specifically, this chapter examines how genetic testing developments have added to the complexity of determining what is in the best interest of the child and presented challenges to the historical precept of presumed fatherhood in the case of married couples. In addition, Appendix A provides a legislative history of provisions related to paternity establishment. This section does not attempt to tackle any of the legal issues concerning parentage that arise from the new reproductive technologies, such as the legal standing of sperm donors, egg donors, or surrogate mothers.

Chapter 1

OVERVIEW

A child born outside of marriage has a biological father but not a legal father. Paternity establishment refers to the legal determination of fatherhood for a child. In 2000, 33.1% of all births in the United States were to unmarried women, adding approximately 1.3 million new children to the list of children needing to have paternity established. Data from the Office of Child Support Enforcement (OCSE) indicate that in 2000 the total number of children in the Child Support Enforcement (CSE) caseload[1] who were born outside of marriage amounted to about 10.1 million. Paternity has been established or acknowledged for about 6.5 million of these children (1.6 million during FY2000), leaving nearly 3.6 million children in the CSE caseload without a legally identified father.

Paternity establishment is not an end in itself, but rather a prerequisite to obtaining ongoing economic support (i.e., child support) from the other (noncustodial) parent.[2] Moreover, in addition to financial benefits, establishing paternity can provide social, psychological, and emotional benefits to the child and in some cases the father's medical history may be needed to give a child proper care.

---

[1] The following families automatically qualify for CSE services (free of charge): families receiving (or who formerly received) Temporary Assistance to Needy Families (TANF) benefits (Title IV-A), foster care payments, or Medicaid coverage. Other families must apply for CSE services, and states must charge an application fee that cannot exceed $25. In FY2000, the CSE caseload consisted of 17.4 million cases, of which 3.3 million were TANF cases; 8.0 million were former-TANF cases, and 6.2 million had never been on TANF.

[2] In 1997 (latest available data), 47% of divorced parents living with children under age 21 whose other parent was not living in the home received child support payments; the comparable statistic for never-married parents was 22%.

Paternity is presumed if a child is conceived within marriage. In other words, the husband is presumed to be the father of a child born to his wife. In cases in which the child is born outside of marriage paternity can be voluntarily acknowledged or it can be contested. It would be contested in cases in which the mother does not want to establish paternity, thereby forcing the father to take his case to court to assert his rights, the biological father does not want to pay child support and denies paternity to delay establishment of a child support order, or the alleged father has genuine doubt about his paternity. If paternity is contested it is generally resolved through either an administrative process or a judicial proceeding.

The public policy interest in paternity establishment is based in part on the dramatic increase in nonmarital births and the economic status of single mothers and their children. The poorest demographic group in the U.S. consists of children in single-parent families. In 2000, 33.1% of all U.S. births were to unmarried women compared to 3.9% in 1950.[3] Moreover, in FY2000, 51.9% of the children in the CSE caseload were born outside of marriage. The percentage of CSE children who were born outside of marriage varied by state, ranging from 7.8% in Kansas (4% in Puerto Rico) to 79.8% in Delaware (see **Table 1**). Concerns about the dependency and poverty of single-parent families led to increased incentives to establish more paternities, financial penalties for failing to establish a specified percentage of paternities, a wide array of enforcement tools with which to collect child support payments, and continued focus on the adequacy of child support payments. In addition, the more recent emphasis on personal responsibility has focused on the benefits of involving noncustodial parents in the lives of their children.

Paternity establishment generally is seen as a means to promote the social goals of (1) providing for the basic financial support of all minor children regardless of the marital status of their parents, (2) ensuring equity in assessing parental liability for the financial support of their children, and (3) promoting responsibility for the consequences of one's actions.[4]

---

[3] Among population groups, the percentage of births to unmarried black women was 68.5% in 2000; the comparable statistics for white women and Hispanic women were 27.1% and 42.5%, respectively.

[4] U.S. Department of Health and Human Services. Office of Child Support Enforcement. *Benefits of Establishing Paternity,* by Laurene T. McKillop with preface by Judith Cassetty. June 1981, reprinted September 1985. p. ix-xii.

> Fathers are an important source of nurturance and emotional security for their infants, as well as a critical source of support for the mother-infant attachment. For the fathers themselves, caring for a child is a transforming experience that often leads to personal growth, motivation, and in turn, improved economic security. As children grow, their fathers' active engagement in their lives enhances their chances for academic success, a healthy gender identity, clear values and moral development, and ultimately greater success in both family and work.
>
> **Source:** Office of Child Support Enforcement, DHHS. *Child Support Report*, v. XXIII, no. 6, June 2000. p.3.

Table 1. CSE Children Born Outside of Marriage, FY2000

State	Number of Children in CSE caseload born out of wedlock	Total Number of children in CSE caseload	Percentage of CSE children born out of wedlock
Alabama	185,983	302,382	61.5
Alaska	8,990	52,166	17.2
Arizona	185,020	283,842	65.2
Arkansas	87,486	174,797	50.1
California	1,527,959	2,388,343	64.0
Colorado	77,258	158,152	48.9
Connecticut	127,638	193,264	66.0
Delaware	49,235	61,734	79.8
District of Columbia	77,498	115,087	67.3
Florida	425,642	932,052	45.7
Georgia	380,637	581,501	65.5
Guam	2,103	19,102	11.0
Hawaii	26,183	92,911	28.2
Idaho	27,635	79,766	34.6
Illinois	840,796	1,148,908	73.2
Indiana	187,704	459,952	40.8
Iowa	106,347	230,803	46.1
Kansas	12,003	154,516	7.8
Kentucky	169,657	395,772	42.9
Louisiana	198,349	350,499	56.6
Maine	38,169	86,601	44.1
Maryland	245,714	339,099	72.5
Massachusetts	114,294	257,708	44.4
Michigan	409,405	1,007,452	40.6

State	Number of Children in CSE caseload born out of wedlock	Total Number of children in CSE caseload	Percentage of CSE children born out of wedlock
Minnesota	142,682	269,697	52.9
Mississippi	204,393	326,036	62.7
Missouri	219,569	524,520	41.9
Montana	17.621	40,998	43.0
Nebraska	42,029	108,831	38.6
Nevada	45,130	143,422	31.5
New Hampshire	14,927	49,019	30.5
New Jersey	186,322	480,529	38.8
New Mexico	13,435	150,845	8.9
New York	629,726	1,163,278	54.1
North Carolina	360,806	532,352	67.8
North Dakota	13,927	32,858	42.4
Ohio	431,352	863,657	49.4
Oklahoma	119,141	176,205	67.6
Oregon	83,623	275,093	30.4
Pennsylvania	240,200	721,913	33.3
Puerto Rico	10,722	267,688	4.0
Rhode Island	45.812	66,623	68.8
South Carolina	171,195	251,516	68.1
South Dakota	11,645	23,632	49.3
Tennessee	175,938	414,517	42.4
Texas	660,604	1,298,459	50.9
Utah	31,453	98,901	31.8
Vermont	11,280	28,386	39.7
Virgin Islands	NA	NA	NA
Virginia	270,038	400,061	67.5
Washington	153,061	365,694	41.9
West Virginia	70,621	138,983	50.8
Wisconsin	194,411	333,762	58.2
Wyoming	14,986	35,530	42.2
Total	**10,098,364**	**19,449,414**	**51.9**

Source: Table prepared by the Congressional Research Service (CRS), based on data from the Office of Child Support Enforcement (OCSE) of the Department of Health and Human Services (HHS).

The federal government reimburses each state 66% of the cost of all allowable expenditures on CSE activities. Allowable expenditures include outlays for locating parents, establishing paternity (at an enhanced matching rate), establishing child support orders, and collecting and distributing payments. In addition to the general federal matching rate of 66%, the federal government provides 90% matching for laboratory costs of genetic testing. Congress justified enhanced funding of genetic tests because paternity establishment is an activity vital to successful child support enforcement.

This book provides background information on paternity establishment, gives a detailed analysis of the paternity establishment process, describes federal CSE and Temporary Assistance to Needy Families (TANF) provisions related to paternity establishment, discusses some policy options to increase the number of paternities established, and examines some of the issues related to the establishment of paternity. In addition, Appendix A provides a legislative history of federal provisions related to paternity establishment.

Chapter 2

PATERNITY ESTABLISHMENT PROCESS

Legally identifying the father is a prerequisite for obtaining a child support order. States generally follow a standard sequence of events in determining paternity. States are required to have procedures which permit the establishment of the paternity of a child at any time before the child reaches age 18.

Although federal CSE law requires states to implement certain administrative processes (e.g., voluntary acknowledgment) to establish paternity, most states use both administrative and judicial methods of paternity establishment. Although the court is generally the final arbiter of deciding paternity in contested cases, the level of court involvement in CSE paternity establishment practices varies. Some states use the courts only for the most difficult contested paternity cases, others require routine judicial approval for all paternity determinations.

According to an HHS Inspector General report, 25 states primarily use quasi-administrative paternity establishment procedures, such as encouraging acknowledgment or other mutual parental consent, often following genetic testing.[5] Quasi-administrative methods primarily rely on the actions and authority of the CSE agency, but also allow limited court involvement. The HHS Inspector General report indicated that the following were characteristic of quasi-administrative procedures: paternity establishment may occur with little or no court involvement; the CSE agency primarily determines the procedures used to determine paternity; voluntary acknowledgment is binding without court approval; genetic tests may be

---

[5] U.S. Department of Health and Human Services. Office of the Inspector General. *Paternity Establishment – Administrative and Judicial Methods.* April 2000, OEI-06-98-00050. p. ii [http://www.dhhs.gov/progorg/oei]

order by the CSE agency without court approval; default orders of paternity may be created with little or no court involvement; and initial hearings and conflict resolution are conducted by the CSE agency.[6] Proponents of the quasi-administrative approach argue that it is easier for parents to understand and for CSE workers to facilitate, and that it is quicker, more routine, and less subjective than judicial procedures.

Before the enactment of the CSE program and the operation of CSE agencies, parents who wanted to establish paternity generally had to hire an attorney and appeal to the courts. State courts still are an integral to the establishment of paternity in many states. The HHS Inspector General report indicates that 26 states primarily use quasi-judicial procedures, under which paternity actions begin and end in the courts. Even under quasi-judicial procedures, the CSE agency generally has the responsibility of shepherding cases through the court system by obtaining initial information on the alleged father, locating absent parents, completing necessary paperwork, and enforcing court mandates. The HHS Inspector General report indicated that the following were characteristic of quasi-judicial procedures: paternity cases require court approval or are often resolved through the courts; state court determines in part the procedures used to establish paternity; voluntary acknowledgment may require court approval prior to initiation of a child support order; genetic testing mandates require a court order; default orders of paternity require a court order; and hearings and conflict resolution are typically conducted by the courts.[7] Proponents of this approach contend that limited involvement of the courts does not slow down the paternity establishment process, and maintain that court action is regarded more seriously by parents and provides a more solid foundation for collection of child support. The Inspector General report found that some states create duplicative processes involving both the courts and the CSE agency that are cumbersome and cause unnecessary delays in the paternity establishment process. It said this occurred, in part because both state CSE agencies and courts may fail to accept administrative paternity establishments as valid.[8]

PRESUMPTIVE PATERNITY FOR MARRIED COUPLES

It is generally the case that if a child is born to a married couple, the wife's husband is presumed to be the baby's father. The precept of presumed

---

[6] *Ibid.*, p. 10.
[7] *Ibid.*, p. 13.
[8] *Ibid.*, p. ii.

fatherhood in the case of a married couple generally is considered to be in the best interest of the child, the stability of marriages, and the public (i.e., child would be less likely to need welfare assistance).[9] The exception occurs when a husband can prove that he is not the biological father of his wife's child by showing that he could not have had intercourse with his wife at the probable time of conception because, for example, he was sterile or impotent, in the military service, or in jail. In these types of situations in which paternity is contested, genetic testing is usually conducted. Courts generally have discouraged paternity cases between married couples unless one of the above exceptions can be proven. For children born outside of marriage, paternity must be acknowledged or established.

VOLUNTARY PATERNITY ACKNOWLEDGMENT

State experience and several studies have shown that many men will voluntarily acknowledge paternity if given the opportunity. When paternity is established voluntarily with the cooperation of both parents, the cost, conflict, and delays of contested cases can be avoided. The voluntary acknowledgment process is available at any time to any father who wants to voluntarily acknowledge paternity. Even if a man is initially reluctant to voluntarily acknowledge parentage because he is unsure whether he actually is the father, he may be willing to do so after receiving genetic test results which indicate a high probability of paternity. Thus, it has proven to be very beneficial for states to provide fathers with multiple opportunities to voluntarily acknowledge paternity.

Federal CSE law requires states to have laws and procedures for a simple civil process for voluntarily acknowledging paternity. Under such a process, the state is required to ensure that the rights and responsibilities of acknowledging paternity are explained to both parents and that due process safeguards are afforded to both parents. States may choose various simple civil methods for obtaining voluntary acknowledgments. The statute requires that voluntary acknowledgment procedures include hospital-based programs that focus on the period immediately before or after the birth of a child.

Each state is required to use a paternity acknowledgment affidavit that includes, at a minimum, the current full name of mother, father and child; Social Security number of mother and father; date of birth of mother, father

---

[9] Center for Law and Social Policy. *Biology and Beyond: The Case for Passage of the New Uniform Parentage Act,* by Paula Roberts with assistance from Nicole Williams. October 2000. p. 14.

and child; address of mother and father; birthplace of the child; a brief explanation of the legal significance of signing a voluntary paternity affidavit and a statement that both parents have 60 days to rescind the paternity acknowledgment affidavit; a clear statement signed by both parents indicating they understand that signing the paternity acknowledgment affidavit is voluntary and that they understand their rights, responsibilities, the alternatives and consequences; signature lines for mother and father; and signature lines for witnesses or notaries.

These requirements are meant to ensure that states' voluntary acknowledgments share certain common elements. If every voluntary acknowledgment contains these basic elements, states will be able to legally recognize and act upon acknowledgments obtained in other states, which should improve interstate case processing. A state is required to give "full faith and credit" to acknowledgments signed in other states if they contain the information required by federal standards and that have been filed in compliance with the procedures required by the state in which they were signed.[10] In addition, the Social Security numbers and addresses may provide valuable information to help locate noncustodial parents and help identify income sources.

States are required to have laws and procedures for filing voluntary acknowledgments with either the state CSE agency or a centralized state agency that provides the state CSE agency access to copies of, and identifying information on, the acknowledgments. If the agency is not the CSE agency, it may be the vital statistics agency, a registry of putative fathers, or some other type of registry or agency. Instead of allowing a state to have multiple filing agencies (such as local courts), federal law requires that the filing agency be a centralized entity so that it will be easier to match acknowledgments with CSE cases and to control access to the acknowledgments.

The 1996 welfare reform law also stipulated that in the case of unmarried parents, the father's name shall not appear on the birth certificate unless he has signed a voluntary acknowledgment or a court has issued an adjudication of paternity.

---

[10] Section 466(a)5(C)(iv) of the Social Security Act requires states to implement laws that require the state to develop and use an affidavit for the voluntary acknowledgment of paternity which includes minimum specified requirements, and to give full faith and credit to such an affidavit signed in any other state according to its procedures. "Full faith and credit" means that a valid affidavit is enforceable where it is issued and in all other jurisdictions.

The National Women's Law Center and the Center on Fathers have cautioned that paternity establishment may have legal consequences outside of child support:

> In addition to having information about the direct consequences of paternity establishment, both parents need to be aware that, in certain circumstances, establishing paternity may have legal consequences that are unrelated to the issue of child support, custody and visitation. Staff who are involved in voluntary paternity establishment need to be aware of these consequences and alert parents to them. For example, the establishment of paternity may, in some states, impose liability for child support on a child's grandparents. A mother who is seeking TANF assistance while cohabiting with the father of her child may be committing, under certain circumstances, an act of welfare fraud. Establishing paternity may in some cases alert law enforcement authorities to the location of individuals who are being sought under a warrant. Establishing paternity may subject some parents to charges of statutory rape. Establishing paternity may prevent some parents from successfully adjusting their immigration status.[11]

CONTESTED PATERNITY

In cases where paternity is not voluntarily acknowledged, the mother of a child generally will make an allegation of paternity to either the court or the CSE agency.[12] The CSE agency generally will locate the alleged father and bring him to court or before an administrative agency where he can either acknowledge or dispute paternity.[13] If a man claims he is not the father, the court or administrative agency can require that he submit to

---

[11] National Women's Law Center and the Center on Fathers, Families, and Public Policy. *Family Ties: Improving Paternity Establishment Practices and Procedures for Low-Income Mothers, Fathers, and Children.* November 2000. p. 18 and 23. **Note:** One consequence of the "good moral character" test for becoming a U.S. citizen is that it encourages the mother to seek paternity establishment, but can discourage a low-income father from admitting paternity, especially if he does not have the financial ability to pay child support, because not paying child support is equated with lacking "good moral character."

[12] In cases in which the mother is receiving CSE services (regardless of whether or not she is on welfare (TANF)), the CSE agency will initiate contact with the alleged father administratively or through the courts after the mother has provided the requested information regarding the child's father. In non-CSE cases, the mother would provide the information to the court (generally via an attorney).

[13] The CSE agency need not attempt to establish paternity in any case involving incest or forcible rape, or in any case in which legal proceedings for adoption are pending, if, in the opinion of the CSE agency, it would not be in the best interests of the child to establish paternity.

parentage (i.e., genetic) testing to establish the probability that he is the father. Through the use of genetic testing techniques, a man may be excluded as a possible biological father, in which case no further action against him is warranted.

If the putative (alleged) father is not excluded on the basis of the scientific test results, authorities still may conclude on the basis of witnesses, resemblance, and other evidence that they do not have sufficient evidence to establish paternity and, therefore drop the paternity allegation. Tests resulting in nonexclusion may serve to convince the putative father that he is, in fact, the father. If this occurs, a voluntary admission often leads to a formal court order. When authorities believe there is enough evidence to support the mother's allegation, but the putative father continues to deny the paternity charges, the case proceeds to a formal adjudication of paternity in a court of law. Using the results of the blood tests and other evidence, the court or the CSE agency, often through an administrative process, may dismiss the case or enter an order of paternity, a prerequisite to obtaining a court order requiring a noncustodial parent to pay child support.

GENETIC TESTS

Most states use one or more of several scientific methods for establishing paternity. These include: red blood cell antigen testing, human leukocyte antigen (HLA) testing, red cell enzyme and serum protein electrophoresis, and deoxyribonucleic acid (DNA) testing.[14] The 1996 welfare reform law mandates that states have and use procedures by which genetic test results can be admitted as evidence of paternity without the need for additional testimony or other proof of accuracy (unless an objection is made). For states to take advantage of this procedure in contested cases, the test must be of a type generally acknowledged as reliable by an HHS-approved accreditation body and be performed by a laboratory approved by the accreditation body.[15] The laboratory is required to issue a report

---

[14] U.S. Department of Health and Human Services. Office of Child Support Enforcement. *Genetic Testing for Paternity Establishment.* September 1993.

[15] State CSE agencies are required to contract with genetic testing laboratories to perform paternity tests to resolve disputed paternity of children born to unmarried parents. The laboratory must perform, at reasonable costs, tests that are legally and medically acceptable for identifying or excluding an alleged father. In support of this effort, the Office of Child Support Enforcement (OCSE) has compiled the fourth edition of the *Directory of Genetic Testing Laboratories* which was disseminated to states in November 2000. The purpose of the directory is to help states identify laboratories which perform legally and medically acceptable genetic tests at reasonable costs.

accompanied by documentation that establishes the chain of custody of the specimens.

Genetic tests generally are performed on small samples of blood collected from the mother, the child, and the alleged father. There are two types of testing procedures for paternity cases: (1) probability of exclusion tests, and (2) probability of paternity tests. Probability of exclusion testing can exclude 95%-99% of falsely-accused men. In other words, the test generally is able to determine that a man is "not" the father of a given child.[16] Thus, there is a very high probability the test will exonerate a falsely-accused man. The exclusion probability has nothing to do with the likelihood that a nonexcluded man may be the father. Probability of paternity testing examines the similarities between the alleged father's blood and the child's and a calculation is made regarding the statistical likelihood of paternity based on the chance of such similarities occurring in a random male in the general population. Probability of paternity testing generally can determine with almost 100% probability that a man is the father of a given child.

Given that questions regarding paternity essentially can be answered scientifically, it is important that the verification process include available advanced scientific technology. Most experts now agree that use of highly reliable DNA tests greatly increases the likelihood of correct identification of putative fathers, DNA tests can be used either to exclude unlikely fathers or to establish a high likelihood that a given man is the father of a child. DNA profiling allows for direct examination of the genetic material that a child inherited from its biological parents. During the testing process, the genetic characteristics of a child are first compared to those of his or her mother. The characteristics that cannot be found in the mother must have been inherited from the biological father. If the tested man does not contain the genetic characteristics necessary to be the biological father of the child, he is excluded. If the DNA of the tested man does contain those genetic characteristics, then the man cannot be excluded and the probability that the tested man is the true biological father can be calculated. One expert, speaking at a child support conference, summed up the effectiveness of DNA testing as follows:

> The DNA fingerprinting technique promises far superior reliability than current blood grouping or human leukocyte antigen analyses. The probability of an unrelated individual sharing the same patterns is

---

[16] If, for example, the rate of exclusion is 95% and the alleged father cannot be excluded, he must fall within the 5% of the population who could have, with the mother in the case, produced a child with the unique genetic makeup shown by the testing.

practically zero. The "DNA fingerprinting" test, developed in England in 1985, refines the favorable statistics to an even greater degree, reducing the probability that two unrelated individuals will have the same DNA fingerprint to one in a quadrillion.[17]

DNA testing is an improvement over other forms of testing because the laboratory technician can (1) use samples from fetuses, newborns or corpses (in HLA testing, one must wait 6 to 12 months after a child is born before testing the child's immunological system); (2) use samples that are over 48 hours old; (3) use smaller samples that can come from a greater variety of body parts (tissue, blood, and hair versus blood only); and (4) achieve a higher level of statistical confidence in the conclusions reached.[18]

Federal law requires states to implement procedures which create a rebuttable or, at the option of the state, conclusive presumption of paternity upon genetic testing results indicating a threshold probability of the alleged father being the father of the child. DNA testing can result in a paternity probability of 99.9%,[19] making most arguments by putative fathers to rebut test results unconvincing.

The state CSE agency has the power (without the need for permission from a court or administrative tribunal) to order genetic tests in appropriate CSE cases. These CSE agencies also must recognize and enforce the ability of other state CSE agencies to take such actions. In any case in which the CSE agency ordered the tests, the state must pay the initial costs. The state is allowed to recoup the cost from the father if paternity is established. If the original test result is contested, further testing can be ordered by the CSE agency if the contestant pays the cost in advance.

Genetic testing for the child, mother, and alleged father usually costs between $300-$700. Once all of the specimens (blood samples) have been received at the laboratory, it generally takes about two weeks before the results are available. The federal government reimburses each state 90% of the laboratory costs of establishing paternity; non-laboratory costs associated with paternity establishment are reimbursed at the general 66% federal matching rate. In FY2000, states in the aggregate spent $32.2 million on laboratory tests associated with the process of determining paternity.

---

[17] Georgeson, L.M. *DNA in Paternity Cases.* Paper presented at the American Bar Association Third National Child support Conference, Arlington, VA, May 1989. p. 568.
[18] U.S. Commission on Interstate Child Support. *Supporting Our Children: A Blueprint for Reform.* 1992. p. 133.
[19] When siblings are named, multiple tests may have to be performed to achieve this level of accuracy and if identical siblings are parties in the paternity suit certainty may never be resolved based on test results alone.

According to a 1999 HHS Inspector General report, some CSE agencies practice the following procedures to eliminate or remove barriers to the effective use of genetic testing: (1) collection of DNA samples from child, alleged father, and mother at the local CSE office, thereby avoiding future delays and transportation problems; and (2) use of buccal swab (i.e., cheek cells) sampling, instead of drawing blood, thereby alleviating some clients' fear of needles as a barrier to genetic testing. In addition, to eliminate expense as a concern for putative fathers' use of genetic testing, some states do not seek to recoup testing costs, or they allow local staff discretion to waive recoupment. However, few areas in the country appear to use all of these strategies.[20]

Widespread availability of inexpensive and reliable genetic tests streamlines paternity establishment by reducing the need for extensive fact finding and minimizing drawn-out litigation. This helps states establish support orders for more children and ensure that the obligor (i.e., person owing child support) really is the child's biological father. However, it also should be noted that advances in genetic testing have contributed to an unanticipated increase in disestablishment actions. While most courts are reluctant to disturb the marital presumption of paternity, some are willing to vacate an order that determines the paternity of an out-of-wedlock child when genetic test evidence later shows that the legal father is not the child's biological father.[21]

---

[20] U.S. Department of Health and Human Services. Office of the Inspector General. *Paternity Establishment – State Use of Genetic Testing.* September 1999, OEI-06-98-00054.

[21] Office of Child Support Enforcement (OCSE). *OCSE Litigation Report, Chapter 4. Paternity Litigation.* [www.dhhs.gov/programs/cse/pubs/reports/litigation/ch04.html] p. 2 of 17.

Chapter 3

PATERNITY PROVISIONS IN THE CSE PROGRAM

The CSE program, enacted in 1975 under title IV-D of the Social Security Act (P.L. 93-647), was established largely because Congress was concerned about the close connection between welfare dependency and the absence of fathers. The Senate Finance Committee report on H.R. 17045, which included child support enforcement provisions that subsequently became the basis of the CSE law, contained the following statements.

> The Committee is concerned at the extent to which the dependency on AFDC is a result of the increasing number of children on the rolls who were born out of wedlock and for whom parental support is not being provided because the identity of the father has not been determined. The Committee believes that an AFDC child has a right to have its paternity ascertained in a fair and efficient manner unless identification of the father is clearly against the best interests of the child. Although this may in some cases conflict with what a social worker considers the mothers' short-term interests, the Committee feels that the child's right to support, inheritance, and to know who his father is deserves the higher social priority.[22]

The main goals of the CSE program are to reduce spending on actual and potential recipients of public welfare by obtaining support from noncustodial parents on an ongoing basis; and to establish paternity for children born outside of marriage so that child support can be obtained. All

---

[22] U.S. Congress. Senate. Committee on Finance. *Social Services Amendments of 1974, report to accompany H.R. 17045.* Senate Report No. 93-1356. p. 51.

50 states, the District of Columbia, Guam, Puerto Rico, and the Virgin Islands operate CSE programs and are entitled to federal matching funds.

Federal CSE law, which applies to all welfare (TANF) families and also to non-welfare families who apply for CSE services, generally (1) requires that paternity be established for 90% of the CSE cases needing such a determination (up from the 50% level set in 1988 and the 75% level set in 1993), (2) establishes a simple civil process for establishing paternity, (3) requires a uniform affidavit to be completed by men voluntarily acknowledging paternity and entitles such affidavits to full faith and credit in any state, (4) stipulates that a signed acknowledgment of paternity be considered a legal finding of paternity unless rescinded within 60 days, and thereafter may be challenged in court only on the basis of fraud, duress, or material mistake of fact, (5) provides that no judicial or administrative action is needed to ratify an acknowledgment that is not challenged, (6) requires all parties to submit to genetic testing in contested paternity cases, and (7) authorizes the establishment of paternity for any child under age 18 who does not have a legally identified father.

PATERNITY ESTABLISHMENT REQUIREMENTS

As noted above, states are required to meet federal standards for the establishment of paternity (Section 452(g) of the Social Security Act). In determining compliance, a state may use as its paternity establishment percentage either (1) the state's CSE paternity establishment percentage or (2) the state's statewide paternity establishment percentage.

The state CSE paternity establishment percentage is based on the entire number of children in the CSE caseload who had been born out of wedlock, regardless of year of birth, and whether paternity had been established for them; whereas, the state's statewide paternity establishment percentage is based on births and paternities established in a single year.

The state's CSE paternity establishment percentage is obtained by dividing the total number of children in the state's CSE caseload in the fiscal year who were born out of wedlock, and for whom paternity has been established or acknowledged by the total number of children in the state's CSE caseload at the end of the preceding fiscal year who are born out of wedlock (regardless of year of birth). For example, in FY2000, there were 987,267 children in California's CSE program who had been born outside of marriage and also had paternity established on their behalf, and at the end of FY1999, there were 1,527,959 children in California's CSE program who had been born outside of marriage. California's CSE paternity establishment percentage was therefore 64.6% in FY2000. In other words, 64.6% of the children in California's CSE program who had been born outside of marriage had legally-identified fathers in FY2000.

The state's statewide paternity establishment percentage is obtained by dividing the total number of minor children in the state who were born out of wedlock and for whom paternity has been established or acknowledged *during* the fiscal year by the total number of children in the state who were born out of wedlock *during* the preceding fiscal year. For example, during FY2000, paternity was established or acknowledged for 306,508 children born in FY2000 in California; whereas, during FY1999, 170,607 children were born outside of marriage in California. California's statewide paternity establishment percentage was thereby 179.7% in FY2000. In other words, the number of paternities established in California in FY2000 for children born in FY2000 exceeded the number of children than were born out of wedlock in FY1999.

To meet federal requirements, the paternity establishment percentage in a state must exceed or equal 90% or, for states with lower percentages, must show specified levels of improvement compared to the previous year –

- for a state with a paternity establishment percentage of not less than 75% but less than 90% for such fiscal year, the paternity establishment percentage of the state for the immediately preceding fiscal year plus 2 percentage points;

- for a state with a paternity establishment percentage of not less than 50% but less than 75% for such fiscal year, the paternity establishment percentage of the state for the immediately preceding fiscal year plus 3 percentage points;

- for a state with a paternity establishment percentage of not less than 45% but less than 50% for such fiscal year, the paternity establishment percentage of the state for the immediately preceding fiscal year plus 4 percentage points;

- for a state with a paternity establishment percentage of not less than 40% but less than 45% for such fiscal year, the paternity establishment percentage of the state for the immediately preceding fiscal year plus 5 percentage points;

- for a state with a paternity establishment percentage of less than 40% for such fiscal year, the paternity establishment percentage of the state for the immediately preceding fiscal year plus 6 percentage points.

In FY2000, the CSE paternity establishment percentage for the nation as a whole was 64.7%. The range among the states went from a high of 100% in Montana to a low of 31.7% in the District of Columbia (32.6% in New Mexico). In FY2000, the statewide paternity establishment percentage for the nation as a whole was 89.8%. The range among the states went from a high of 179.7% in California to a low of 32.3% in Alabama. Data not available for 18 states (see **Table 2,** Percentage of Paternities Established Through the CSE Program and Statewide, FY2000).

Table 2. **Paternities Established throughout the CSE Program and Statewide, FY2000**

State	CSE paternities established or acknowledged (regardless of year established)	CSE out-of-wedlock births (regardless of year of birth)	Percentage of CSE Paternities established	Statewide paternities established or acknowledged (in FY2000)	Statewide out-of-wedlock births (in FY1999)	Percent of statewide paternities established
Alabama	110,940	185,983	59.7	6,689	20,693	32.3
Alaska	6,758	8,990	75.2	2,987	3,239	92.2
Arizona	141,108	185,020	76.3	NA	31,264	NA
Arkansas	56,634	87,486	64.7	NA	4,535	NA
California	987,267	1,527,959	64.6	306,508	170,607	179.7
Colorado	66,895	77,258	86.6	14,635	16,048	91.2
Connecticut	91,724	127,638	71.9	13,287	12,259	106.6
Delaware	33,359	49,235	67.8	NA	4,111	NA
District of Columbia	24,551	77,498	31.7	4,343	6,517	66.6
Florida	366,915	425,642	86.2	60,531	77,069	78.5
Georgia	185,765	380,637	48.8	NA	NA	NA
Guam	689	2,103	32.8	1,885	2,010	93.8
Hawaii	22,476	26,183	85.8	NA	11,585	NA
Idaho	23,080	27,635	83.5	2,660	4,284	62.1
Illinois	319,727	840,796	38.0	52,894	57,079	92.7
Indiana	70,492	187,704	37.6	NA	NA	NA
Iowa	85,874	106,347	80.7	9,522	9,853	96.6
Kansas	7,002	12,003	58.3	8,571	10,986	78.0
Kentucky	114,327	169,657	67.4	7,993	7,810	102.3
Louisiana	118,916	198,349	60.0	14,286	NA	NA
Maine	33,750	38,169	88.4	2,905	3,815	76.1
Maryland	177,209	245,714	72.1	33,182	231,138	14.4
Massachusetts	89,154	114,294	78.0	22,084	21,202	104.2

State	CSE paternities established or acknowledged (regardless of year established)	CSE out-of-wedlock births (regardless of year of birth)	Percentage of CSE Paternities established	Statewide paternities established or acknowledged (in FY2000)	Statewide out-of-wedlock births (in FY1999)	Percent of statewide paternities established
Michigan	311,239	409,405	76.0	41,372	41,317	100.1
Minnesota	130,764	142,682	72.7	14,562	16,873	86.3
Mississippi	131,315	204,393	64.2	NA	NA	NA
Missouri	166,199	219,569	75.7	22,242	26,390	84.3
Montana	17,631	17,621	100.1	NA	2,983	NA
Nebraska	31,696	42,029	75.4	5,451	6,326	86.2
Nevada	33,674	45,130	74.6	NA	NA	NA
New Hampshire	13,269	14,937	88.8	3,248	3,477	93.4
New Jersey	136,717	186,322	73.4	34,781	31,214	111.4
New Mexico	4,376	13,435	32.6	11,996	11,525	104.1
New York	393,432	629,726	62.5	97,874	94,687	103.4
North Carolina	196,027	360,806	54.3	NA	NA	NA
North Dakota	10,973	13,927	78.8	NA	2,425	NA
Ohio	322,104	431,351	74.7	56,684	51,910	109.2
Oklahoma	43,049	119,141	36.1	13,344	16,092	82.9
Oregon	55,750	83,623	66.7	12,246	14,315	85.5
Pennsylvania	182,714	240,200	76.1	56.588	47,585	118.9
Puerto Rico	9,002	10,722	84.0	27,387	29,591	92.6
Rhode Island	27,410	45,812	59.8	NA	NA	NA
South Carolina	124,014	171,195	72.4	11,687	20,271	57.7
South Dakota	10,663	11,645	91.6	NA	3,324	NA
Tennessee	111,133	175,938	63.2	19,150	28,111	68.1
Texas	342,082	660,604	51.8	115,642	101,479	114.0
Utah	30,024	31,453	95.5	7,213	8,024	89.9
Vermont	10,035	11,280	89.0	NA	NA	NA
Virgin Islands	NA	NA	NA	1,148	NA	NA
Virginia	221,951	270,038	82.2	23,449	27,985	83.8
Washington	144,898	153,061	94.7	NA	21,978	NA
West Virginia	52,531	70,621	74.4	6,210	6,673	93.1
Wisconsin	153,808	194,411	79.1	NA	NA	NA
Wyoming	8,996	14,986	60.0	1,805	1,773	101.8
Total	6,535,088	10,098,364	64.7	1,149,041	1,279,922	89.8

Source: Table prepared by the Congressional Research Service (CRS), based on data from the Office of Child Support Enforcement (OCSE) of the Department of Health and Human Services (HHS).

Note: State paternity acknowledgments include an unknown number of acknowledgments for children in the CSE caseload.

Penalty for Noncompliance

Federal CSE law requires states to meet federal standards for the establishment of paternity. If an audit finds that the state CSE program has not substantially complied with those standards, the state is subject to a penalty (not the so-called "nuclear" penalty described in footnote 25, but a specified lesser penalty). In accordance with this penalty, the HHS Secretary must reduce a state's TANF block grant payment by not less than 1% nor more than 2% for the first failure to comply; by not less than 2% nor more than 3% for the second consecutive failure to comply; and by not less than 3% nor more than 5% for the third or subsequent consecutive failure to comply.

Program Incentives for Paternity Establishment

The Personal Responsibility and Work Opportunity Reconciliation Act of 1996, P.L. 104-193, required the Secretary of HHS in consultation with the state CSE directors to develop a revenue-neutral system of incentive payments to states that is based on performance.[23] The incentive system is based on the state's performance in five major areas of child support enforcement: establishment of paternities, establishment of child support orders, collections on current child support payments, collections on past-due child support (i.e., arrearages), and cost-effectiveness. Each of the measures is translated into a mathematical formula. The amount of incentive payments for a particular measure is based on established standards of performance. For each standard, there is an upper threshold. All states that achieve performance levels at or above this upper threshold are entitled to a portion of a maximum possible incentive for that performance measure. Simultaneously, there is a minimum level of performance below which states are not paid an incentive, unless the state has improved significantly over its previous year's performance.

One of the main reasons for mandating a new incentive payment system was that the old system was based almost entirely on child support

---

[23] The total amount of the incentive payment depends on four factors: the total amount of money available in a given fiscal year from which to make incentive payments, the state's success in making collections on behalf of its caseload, the state's performance in five areas (i.e., establishment of paternity and child support orders, collections of current and past-due support payments, and cost-effectiveness), and the relative success or failure of other states in making collections and meeting these performance criteria. Federal law (P.L. 105-200, enacted July 16, 1998) stipulated that the incentive payment pool cannot exceed specified amounts, i.e., $422 million for FY2000, $429 million for FY2001; $450 million for FY2002; $461 million for FY2003; $454 million for FY2004; $446 million for FY2005; $458 million for FY2006; $471 million for FY2007; $483 million for FY2008. For years after FY2008, the incentive pool is required to be increased to account for inflation.

collections. Congress contended that an approach was needed to reward both collections and state performance on the underlying factors on which collections were based. Thus, one of the "performances" rewarded by the new incentive payment system is paternity establishment. Under the new incentive system, if a state had a paternity establishment percentage of 80% or higher, the state would be eligible for 100% of the maximum value of the incentive. The maximum incentive would be based on a percentage of the individual state's collections. If a state had a paternity establishment percentage of 49% or lower, the state would have to increase its paternity establishment percentage by at least 10 percentage points over its prior year's performance in order to receive an incentive. If the state made such an improvement it would be eligible for 50% of the state's maximum incentive amount.

During the development of the new incentive system, concern was expressed about the possibility that states would be financially penalized for noncompliance with federal requirements at the same time they were eligible for CSE incentive payments. Some analysts argued that the lack of an incentive payment would make states subject to a double penalty if they did not improve performance. It was decided that states should be eligible for incentives based on performance even if they were subject to penalties because their performance had not improved to the extent required to avoid the penalty. The following rationale was cited by a working group that included HHS staff and CSE directors to help the HHS Secretary make recommendations on a new CSE incentive payment system.

> If a state is at an 85% performance level one year, and increases to 86% the following year, it would be subject to a penalty for not achieving a 2% increase in performance. The Incentive Funding Work Group felt that the state should be rewarded for its high level of performance by receiving 100% of the possible incentive to encourage sustained performance. The paternity incentive is an integral part of the recognition and reward of state performance in the range of required program results, and, as such, merits distinction regardless of the potential for a penalty.[24]

---

[24] Incentive Funding Working Group. Report to the Secretary of Health and Human Services. January 31, 1997. p. 9.

Chapter 4

PATERNITY/FATHERHOOD PROVISIONS IN THE TANF PROGRAM

Federal law requires every state operating a TANF program to also operate a CSE program.[25] It also requires applicants for, and recipients of, TANF to assign their rights to child support to the state in order to receive TANF benefits. In addition, each applicant or recipient of TANF must cooperate with the state to establish the paternity of a child born outside of marriage and to obtain child support payments. Further, a 1999 HHS directive regarding the statutory goal of the TANF program to promote the formation and maintenance of two-parent families, interpreted two-parent families to mean not only married-couple families, but also never-married, separated, and divorced parents, whether living together or not. Thus, many states classify their fatherhood programs and programs that encourage visitation by noncustodial parents under the rubric of fulfilling the purposes of the TANF program.

---

[25] Under federal law, if a state fails to implement the CSE state plan requirements (Sections 454 and 466 of the Social Security Act), the Office of Child Support Enforcement (OCSE) cannot approve the state's CSE program. Under the law, disapproval of a state's CSE plan requires suspension of all federal CSE payments, after an appeals process. Moreover, the TANF title of P.L. 104-193 provides that the Governor of a state must certify that he or she will operate an approved CSE program as a condition of eligibility for a TANF block grant. Thus, if a state did not comply with the CSE procedures concerning paternity establishment (Section 466(a)(5) of the Social Security Act), it could be in jeopardy of losing its federal CSE funding. If a state has to update its TANF plan while the state's CSE plan is in disapproval status, that state's TANF block grant funds also would be in jeopardy.

COOPERATION REQUIREMENTS

Legally identifying the father is a prerequisite for obtaining a child support order. Federal law requires TANF block grant (Title IV-A) applicants and recipients, as a condition of receiving cash benefits, to cooperate in establishing paternity or obtaining support payments. Moreover, it imposes a penalty for noncooperation; if it is determined that an individual is not cooperating, and the individual does not qualify for any good cause or other exception, then the state must reduce the family's TANF benefit by at least 25%, and may remove the family from the TANF program.

Pursuant to the 1996 welfare reform law (P.L. 104-193), Section 454(29) of the Social Security Act requires that parents must cooperate "in good faith" with the state CSE agency in establishing paternity, or in establishing, modifying, or enforcing a child support order. P.L. 104-193 required the custodial parent to (1) name the other parent, subject to good cause and other exceptions, (2) supply additional necessary information and appear at interviews, hearings, and legal proceedings, and (3) submit (together with the child) to genetic tests that are ordered by a judge or administrative agency. Unlike prior AFDC law, the CSE agency, not the Title IV-A agency, is responsible for making the cooperation determination. The CSE agency also is required to promptly notify the individual and the TANF agency, the Foster Care agency, the Medicaid agency, or the Food Stamp agency of a noncooperation determination. Upon receiving such a notification, the appropriate agency must sanction the family for noncooperation, unless the individual qualifies for a "good cause" or other exemption. As noted above, in a TANF case, the state must reduce the family's TANF benefit by at least 25% and may remove the family from the TANF program. If a state fails to promptly impose a sanction on the family, the state would be subject to a reduction of from 1% to 5% of its TANF block grant funds. Under federal law, the CSE agency has the authority to determine "good cause" and other exceptions from the cooperation requirement. Federal law authorizes the states, rather than the federal government, to develop "good cause" and other exceptions to the cooperation requirement.

FATHERHOOD INITIATIVES

Many policymakers maintain that the children in single-parent families need more than a working mother and sporadic child support.[26] They see the next step in welfare reform as engaging fathers in the lives of the children. Federal, state, and local governments along with public and private organizations are supporting programs and activities that promote the financial and personal responsibility of noncustodial fathers to their children and increase contact of fathers with their children. These programs have come to be known as "fatherhood" programs or initiatives. The following 14 states report that they have, or plan to have, fatherhood initiatives: Alabama, Arizona, Florida, Georgia, Indiana, Maryland, Minnesota, Mississippi, Missouri, North Carolina, Pennsylvania, Tennessee, Virginia, and Wisconsin. An HHS-funded study on several fatherhood demonstration projects is currently underway.

Most fatherhood programs include media campaigns that emphasize the importance of emotional, physical, psychological, and financial connections of fathers to their children. Most fatherhood programs include parenting education; guidance in responsible decision-making; mediation services for both parents; information about the purposes of the CSE program, and how it works; counseling or classes related to conflict resolution, coping with stress, and problem-solving skills; peer support; and job training opportunities (skills development, interviewing skills, job search, job retention skills, job advancement skills, etc.).

During the 106th Congress, legislation was twice passed by the House that would have authorized funding for a national fatherhood competitive grant program. Although a national responsible fatherhood program was not enacted, for FY2001 Congress appropriated $3.5 million for a national fatherhood organization named the National Fatherhood Initiative and $500,000 for an organization called the Institute for Responsible Fatherhood and Family Revitalization (P.L. 106-553 and P.L. 106-554).

---

[26] The 1996 welfare reform law (P.L. 104-193) supported the participation of fathers in the lives of their children through an annual $10 million entitlement of CSE funds to states to establish and operate access and visitation programs. In addition, the Welfare-to-Work grant program was established in 1997 (P.L. 105-33) to help long-term welfare recipients obtain work. P.L. 105-33 appropriated funding for FY1998 and FY1999 for the Welfare-to-Work program and required the Department of Labor to administer the program. The Welfare-to-work grant program was modified in 1999 (P.L. 106-113) to specifically include noncustodial parents who are unemployed, underemployed, or who are having difficulty paying their child support obligations to eligible recipients. P.L. 106-554 gave grantees an additional 2 years to expend funds, allowing Welfare-to-work expenditures (which would otherwise expire in FY2002) to continue through FY2004.

Although the federal government does not currently provide *specifically* for fatherhood programs, many states and localities, private organizations and nonprofit agencies operate fatherhood programs. Current programs that have somewhat broad funding authority that enable them to include funding for fatherhood initiatives include the Temporary Assistance for Needy Families (TANF) program, TANF state Maintenance-of-Effort (MOE) funding, welfare-to-work funds, Child Support Enforcement (CSE) funds, and Social Services Block Grant (Title XX) funds (for information on responsible fatherhood legislation in the 107th Congress, see discussion below on Fatherhood Grant Programs).

TANF MARRIAGE AND TWO-PARENT FAMILY GOALS

The TANF block grant program established statutory goals to promote the formation and maintenance of two-parent families and to reduce welfare dependence via job preparation, work, and marriage. States may spend TANF funds on a wide range of activities (services) for cash welfare recipients and other families toward the achievement of these goals. Beginning in FY2002, a portion of the TANF "high performance bonus" ($10 million) will go to the 10 states with the greatest increase in the percent of children living in married-couple families.[27]

Years before the TANF program was enacted, some child support advocates recommended that the primary focus for paternity actions be directed towards maximizing the day-to-day involvement of the father in paternity cases. They argued that federal assistance should be oriented toward helping recipients to become self-sufficient and toward encouraging family formation. They recommended decriminalizing and minimizing the adversarial nature of domestic relations and paternity proceedings and the need to give priority to access/visitation, rather than collection. They

---

[27] The TANF program awards "high performance" bonuses to states that rank high on outcome measures related to the program's goals. A total of $1 billion was provided for 5 years (averaging $200 million per year) for this bonus.

maintained that in the long run this would benefit parents, children, and federal support obligations.[28]

---

[28] U.S. Commission on Interstate Child Support. Minority Report. *Let the Fathers Return,* by Don Chavez, 1992. p. 24.

Chapter 5

POLICY OPTIONS TO INCREASE THE LEVEL OF PATERNITY ESTABLISHMENT

If examined in isolation, the CSE program has made great strides in establishing paternity. Between FY1977 and FY2000 the number of children in the CSE program whose paternity was established (or acknowledged) increased by 2,179%, from 68,263 in FY1977 to 1,555,581 in FY2000. However, if examined in the context of all the children in the CSE caseload who need a paternity determination, the CSE performance is less impressive. In FY2000, there were about 10.1 million children in the CSE caseload who were born outside of marriage. Of these children, 6.5 million or 64.7% had paternity established or acknowledged (the comparable percentage for FY1999 was 59.0%).[29]

Even so, with more paternities being established than children being born outside of marriage, progress is being made in reducing the number of children who do not have legally established fathers. As noted above, paternity was established or acknowledged for nearly 1.6 million children in the CSE caseload during FY2000, whereas in FY2000 about 1.3 million babies were born outside of marriage. In some states, establishing paternities for newborns is almost at 100%. However, as the data indicate, establishing paternity for older children is still difficult.

Some proposals or programs that may increase the numbers of paternities established include: more cooperation between parents and the CSE agencies, continued outreach to fathers acknowledging their importance to their children, voluntary acknowledgment of paternity especially via

---

[29] Comparable data are not available for earlier years.

hospital-based programs, and a renewed emphasis on finding the fathers of older children, perhaps through media campaigns.

COOPERATION BETWEEN PARENTS AND CSE AGENCIES

Gaining cooperation from TANF families is important to facilitating child support enforcement. Since the enactment of the CSE program, federal law has stipulated that cash welfare recipients would be obligated to assist states in pursuing support for their children.[30] Generally, states ask for the putative father's full name, Social Security number, driver's license number, date of birth, and current employment data. States may also request the last-known address of the putative father, make and model of putative father's automobile, relatives' addresses, and previous employers. Nonetheless, some TANF mothers are unwilling or hesitant about providing such information because they do not want the father in the child's life, they want to protect the father from child support collection, or they fear domestic violence. The changes made to the cooperation requirement in the 1996 welfare reform law (P.L. 104-193) were in part an attempt to improve the cooperation of custodial parents with the CSE agency (see earlier section on Cooperation Requirements).[31]

Although the CSE program has historically been the policy answer to the problem of father absence, because its focus until recently was exclusively on financial support, it has had the practical effect of alienating many low-income fathers who are unable to meet their child support obligations. Some policy analysts maintain that fathers are in effect devalued when their role in their children's lives is based solely on their cash contributions. They argue that public policies are needed to support the father's role as nurturer, disciplinarian, mentor, and moral instructor.[32]

Some observers maintain that there are several ways to stimulate more cooperation between parents and CSE agencies. First, fully inform parents about the paternity establishment process and its ramifications. They say that

---

[30] With respect to non-welfare clients, it was assumed that they would automatically cooperate with the CSE agency, otherwise they would not have applied for CSE services.

[31] U.S. Department of Health and Human Services. Office of the Inspector General. *Client Cooperation With Child Support Enforcement – Policies and Practices.* March 2000, OEI-06-98-00040. [http://www.dhhs.gov/progorg/oei]

[32] Horn, Wade F., and Isabel V. Sawhill. *Making Room For Daddy: Fathers, Marriage, and Welfare Reform.* Working Paper, The Brookings Institution. April 26, 2001. p. 4.

states should develop educational materials for parents and prospective parents that are sensitive to the issues of race, gender, domestic violence, cultural and socio-economic circumstances and that provide specific and honest information about the rights and responsibilities that accompany paternity establishment. Some analysts argue that child support caseworkers understand the paternity establishment process better than TANF caseworkers and therefore should handle the initial intake interview in TANF cases if paternity is an issue. Some observers contend that states should provide parents who both want to establish paternity with access to a simple and accessible voluntary paternity acknowledgment process, not limited to the hospital setting. They say that staff who provide the information to parents should be properly trained and very knowledgeable about paternity establishment. They state that paternity establishment procedures should be fair in that both parents are afforded their due process rights, and protections against domestic violence are taken into account. Others recommend that Congress eliminate policies that rely on the state's coercive power to mandate paternity establishment against the wishes of both parents (mostly mothers), such as the cooperation and assignment requirements imposed on TANF families.[33]

Some observers maintain that noncustodial parents and the CSE program have irreconcilable differences and that the most that should be expected is (1) for the CSE agency to provide both parents with professional and knowledgeable information and service, and with multiple opportunities to furnish the appropriate information or otherwise cooperate in establishing paternity or in establishing and collecting child support; and (2) for noncustodial parents to clearly understand the purposes of the CSE program, the requirements imposed on custodial parents and noncustodial parents, and that they as noncustodial parents have a moral and societal responsibility to have (to build) a loving relationship with their children.[34] They contend that if the CSE agencies provide honest information in a straightforward manner, they may gain the cooperation of both parents, if not their trust.

---

[33] National Women's Law Center and the Center on Fathers, Families, and Public Policy. *Family Ties: Improving Paternity Establishment Practices and Procedures for Low-Income Mothers, Fathers, and Children.* November 2000. p. 24-28.

[34] University of Wisconsin - Madison. Institute for Research on Poverty. A Failed Relationship? Low-income families and the Child Support enforcement system, by Maureen Waller and Robert Plotnick. *Focus*, v. 21, no. 1, spring 2000. p. 12-17. (Hereafter cited as University of Wisconsin - Madison, A Failed Relationship.)

FATHERHOOD GRANT PROGRAMS

In hopes of improving the long-term outlook for children in single-parent families, federal, state, and local governments along with public and private organizations are supporting programs and activities that promote the financial and personal responsibility of noncustodial fathers to their children and increase the participation of fathers in the lives of their children. To help fathers and mothers meet their parental responsibilities, many policy analysts and observers support broad-based collaborative strategies that go beyond welfare and child support agencies and include schools, work programs, prison systems, churches, community organizations, and the health care system.

P.L. 107-116, the Labor, HHS, Education appropriation bill (H.R. 3061) for FY2002 did not include the Administration's FY2002 fatherhood proposal.[35] However, several pending bills (H.R. 1300/S. 653, H.R. 1471, S. 685, S. 940/H.R. 1990, H.R. 2893, H.R. 3625, H.R. 4090, and H.R. 4737[36]) authorize funding for grant programs for fatherhood initiatives. Moreover, President Bush's FY2003 Budget requests $20 million annually for FY2003-FY2007 for competitive grants to community and faith-based organizations for programs that help noncustodial fathers support their families to avoid or leave cash welfare, become more involved in their children's lives, promote successful parenting, and encourage and support healthy marriages and married fatherhood.

IN-HOSPITAL PATERNITY ESTABLISHMENT

Experience of some states indicated that a father of a child born to an unmarried mother is more likely to be present and to admit paternity during the time surrounding birth than later on. Generally, early paternity

---

[35] President Bush's FY2002 Budget requested $64 million in FY2002 ($315 million over 5 years) for competitive grants to community and faith-based organizations for programs that help unemployed and low-income fathers and their families avoid or leave cash welfare, and programs that promote successful parenting and strengthen marriage, including $4 million to support programs through grants, contracts or cooperative agreements that focus the national attention (through public education and awareness, the use of mass media campaigns, research, etc.) on the benefits of involving fathers in their children's lives.

[36] H.R. 4737, the Personal Responsibility, Work, and Family Promotion Act of 2002, which includes $20 million annually for FY2003-FY2007 for fatherhood programs, was passed by the House on May 16, 2002.

establishment reduces location difficulties and administrative costs which can occur if paternity establishment is delayed.

P.L. 103-66, the Omnibus Budget Reconciliation Act of 1993, required states to have in effect by October 1, 1993, a simple civil process for voluntarily acknowledging paternity under which the state must explain the rights and responsibilities of acknowledging paternity to both parents and afford due process safeguards to both parents. The law stipulated that states had to include a hospital-based program for the voluntary acknowledgment of paternity during the period immediately preceding or following the birth of a child.[37] Congress asserted that a nonadversarial approach at hospitals, prenatal clinics, and birthing centers would probably increase the number of paternities established.

The Colorado Child Support Improvement Project which was implemented in four hospitals in the Denver area during 1992-1994 simplified hospital-based paternity establishment processes by eliminating associated fees and waiting periods and replacing notarized signatures with witnessed ones. In addition, during the demonstration period, birth registration clerks systematically approached all unwed parents and explained the benefits of paternity, and assisted interested fathers in completing paternity affidavits. An evaluation of the demonstration project revealed that these changes nearly doubled voluntary paternity acknowledgment rates. Some analysts note that although several demonstration projects showed a significant increase in acknowledgments following implementation of simplified hospital-based paternity acknowledgment procedures, 50% or more of the alleged fathers refused to sign. Many of these men were involved with women who had more than two children and/or were receiving some form of welfare assistance.[38]

For the nation as a whole, during the 6-year period FY1994-FY2000, in-hospital paternity acknowledgments increased 781%, from 78,129 in FY1994 (first year that data reported to OCSE) to 688,510 in FY2000.

---

[37] Federal law also required the state agency responsible for maintaining birth records to offer voluntary paternity establishment services. Further, it stipulated that the HHS Secretary must prescribe regulations specifying the types of other entities that may offer voluntary paternity establishment services. In addition, the voluntary paternity establishment services program must also be available at other entities designated by the state. Such entities may include: public heath clinics (including Supplementary Feeding Program for Women, Infants, and Children (WIC) and Maternal and Child Health (MCH) clinics); CSE agencies, TANF agencies, Food Stamp agencies; Head Start and child care agencies; Community Action agencies; secondary education schools, particularly those that have parenthood education curricula; and legal aid agencies.

[38] Pearson, Jessica and Nancy Thoennes. *The Child Support Improvement Project: Paternity Establishment,* Center for Policy Research. September 30,1995.

Some analysts attribute the dramatic increase in voluntary acknowledgments via hospital-based programs to the rise in the number of cohabiting families. One study indicates that fathers in cohabiting families generally do not have child support orders and are not required to pay child support because (like married fathers) they are presumed to be contributing financially to their child's or children's care. The author contends that voluntary acknowledgment is less likely for children whose parents are not cohabiting because in those cases once paternity is acknowledged, the state can obligate the father to pay child support.[39]

According to many CSE administrators, in-hospital paternity establishment saves time and tax dollars by eliminating what could be a lengthy process of administrative proceedings, court hearings, and DNA testing. On the other hand, during a series of discussions among researchers, practitioners, and advocates it was noted that the hospital setting has several disadvantages. It was pointed out that current hospital maternity stays are very brief and the period surrounding childbirth is often emotionally stressful. Some discussants thereby maintained that parents are often not emotionally or mentally able to grasp the paternity acknowledgment information presented to them.[40]

Some suggestions for making in-hospital acknowledgment programs more successful include mandating that the paternity acknowledgment procedures and materials from the personnel in vital statistics and CSEs are consistent and complementary; providing training on paternity acknowledgment and its implications to birth registration personnel; generating timely, hospital-specific performance information regarding voluntary paternity acknowledgment; and automating CSE systems so that child support personnel can assess birth certificate information to determine whether paternity needs to be established.[41] Other suggestions include: better training of hospital staff so that they can sufficiently answer parents' questions on the paternity establishment process, the development and distribution by hospitals of culturally sensitive brochures that clearly explain the paternity establishment process (available in different languages), and the inclusion on the voluntary paternity establishment form of information about the effect of voluntary paternity establishment on custody and visitation.[42]

---

[39] Turner, Mark. Child Support Enforcement and In-Hospital Paternity Establishment in Seven Cities. Center for Research on Child Wellbeing. Working Paper #00-22-FF.
[40] National Women's Law Center and the Center on Fathers, Families, and Public Policy. *Family Ties: Improving Paternity Establishment Practices and Procedures for Low-Income Mothers, Fathers, and Children.* November 2000. p. 17.
[41] *Ibid.*, p. 17.
[42] *Ibid.*, p. 17.

IDENTIFYING THE FATHERS OF OLDER CHILDREN

Most researchers and observers agree that the best time to establish voluntary paternity is at the time the child is born and that the probability of establishing paternity declines as children age.

As noted earlier in the chapter, about 1.3 million babies were born to unmarried parents in 2000. In FY2000, the CSE agencies reported nearly 700,000 cases in which paternity was voluntarily acknowledged. Most of these cases involve newborns. In addition, paternity was established for another 900,000 children.

As the child of unmarried parents gets older, contact between his or her parents generally diminishes. It is often the case that mothers lose track of the putative father (e.g., telephone number is disconnected or has been changed and/or he has moved to a new location). Policymakers expect the expanded location capabilities of the CSE agencies, such as the State and National New Hires Directories and other automated directories, to help locate putative fathers of older children much faster than under the previous system.

One approach that many organizations and most states have used to focus attention on fathers' responsibility for older children is media campaigns. Outreach campaigns are usually designed to educate parents and the general public about the benefits of, and the process for, establishing paternity. They try to encourage both mothers and fathers to seek and cooperate with paternity establishment efforts. Many outreach campaigns air public service announcements on the radio and television, display posters, billboards, brochures, pamphlets, and flyers throughout the community or state, provide information booths at selected community events, and give away promotional items such as pens, magnets, and book markers imprinted with the CSE agency's address and telephone number. In addition, the CSE agency may provide special seminars on the benefits of paternity establishment to specified groups. The shaded box below displays several of the slogans that have been used by states and professional sporting organizations to promote the fatherhood message.

Even though it is common knowledge that a child does not necessarily look like either of his or her biological parents, in the case of older children, paternity is more likely to be established in an amicable manner if the child resembles the father or his family. Although blood or genetic testing is the standard procedure in contested paternity cases, many people view such tests as an affront to their integrity and an indication of a lack of trust. This situation is exacerbated in the case of an older child. According to some focus group discussants, for many couples, once one of the partners or alleged partners indicates that a paternity test is needed, any future chance for cooperative parenting is greatly diminished because of lingering animosity over the father not stepping forward and meeting his financial responsibility or the mother not being honest about her use of birth control.[43]

Fatherhood Media Campaign Messages

- Fatherhood Can Be Child's Play – Huddle Up. (NFO – Michigan)
- Step Up to the Plate, Be a Responsible Father (Major League Baseball – California)
- First Things First – An Education, a Job, and Marriage Should Precede Having Children (South Carolina)
- They're Your Kids, Be Their Dad (Ohio, Illinois, Indiana, and Maryland)
- Fatherhood: No Penalty for Holding (NFL – New Jersey)
- Fatherhood is One Responsibility Every Dad Needs to Tackle! (NFL – Michigan)

---

[43] Furstenberg, Frank F. Jr., Kay E. Sherwood, and Mercer L. Sullivan. *Parents' Fair Share Demonstration. Caring and Paying: What Fathers and Mothers Say About Child Support.* Manpower Demonstration Research Corporation. July 1992. p. 47.

Chapter 6

OTHER PATERNITY ISSUES

Although many paternity concerns are intermingled with the effectiveness of the CSE program, some are beyond the scope of the CSE program. This section of the chapter highlights some of these issues. It examines how genetic testing developments have added to the complexity of what is in the best interest of the child and have sometimes disproved the presumption that a husband is the father of his wife's child. It also relays some of the concerns of mothers and alleged fathers with respect to paternity establishment. In addition, it briefly summarizes some of the benefits of paternity establishment for children. This section does not attempt to tackle any of the legal issues concerning parentage that arise from the new reproductive technologies. In other words, there is no discussion of the legal standing of sperm donors, egg donors, or surrogate mothers.[44]

PATERNITY OF MARITAL CHILDREN

During the last several years, advances in genetic testing have resulted in more instances of putative fathers substantiating their claim that they in fact are not the biological father of the child in question. In divorce cases in which the mother contends that her husband is not the father of her child and genetic tests verify her claim, but the husband nevertheless wants to maintain a parent-child relationship and continue the emotional and financial responsibilities of fatherhood, many courts considering the best interests of

---

[44] For information on these types of issues, see *Biology and Beyond: The Case for Passage of the New Uniform Parentage Act,* by Paula Roberts with assistance from Nicole Williams. Center on Law and Social Policy. October 2000.

the child and the public have ruled in the ex-husband's favor, arguing that there is more to fatherhood than biology. In divorce cases in which the husband alleges that children of the marriage are not his and can substantiate his allegation with genetic testing results, some courts have ruled on behalf of the ex-husband, arguing that it is not fair to force a man to assume responsibility for a child to whom he has no biological connection. Other courts have not allowed husbands to raise the paternity issue at divorce, especially if the husband suspected adultery and failed to act, contending that it would not be in the best interest of the child or the public.[45] These examples indicate that in paternity cases the "best interest of the child" doctrine is no longer as clear cut as it once seemed.

FATHERS' RIGHTS AND CONCERNS

Some fatherhood advocates contend that the paternity establishment process is beginning to focus more on efficiency, at the expense of the father's right to due process and his right to representation. They argue that in some instances alleged fathers are not fully informed about the consequences of voluntarily acknowledging paternity and do not fully understand the implication of their statements before they are encouraged to legally acknowledge paternity.

> "While fathers must fulfill their financial commitments, they must also fulfill their emotional commitments. Dads play indispensable roles that cannot be measured in dollars and cents: nurturer, mentor, disciplinarian, moral instructor, and skills coach, among other roles."
>
> **Source:** U.S. Executive Office of the President. A Blueprint for New Beginnings. A Responsible Budget for America's Priorities. Chapter 12. February 2001. p.75.

Information obtained from noncustodial fathers for various surveys and studies consistently tells the same story. Not surprisingly, noncustodial parents, especially low-income fathers, prefer informal child support agreements between themselves and the child's mother wherein they contribute cash support when they can and provide noncash aid such as taking care of the children from time to time and buying food, clothing, presents, etc. as often as they can. This perspective is not new. For years low-income fathers have expressed frustration over not having enough

---

[45] *Ibid.*, p. 14-16.

money to sufficiently provide for their children. Further, many noncustodial fathers maintain that the CSE system is dismissive of their financial condition and continues to pursue child support payments (current as well as arrearages) even when it knows that many of them can barely support themselves. They contend that the CSE program causes conflicts between them and their child's mother because the women often use it as leverage by threatening to report them to CSE authorities, take them back to court, have more of their wages garnished, or have them arrested.[46] One report noted: "Often fathers cannot pay their support, cannot afford activities with their children... If the divorced father...is ordered to pay an amount of support that makes it impossible to meet his own living expenses and pay for visitation activities – he probably will not see much of his children."[47]

Default Judgments

Federal law requires states to have procedures requiring a default order to be entered in a paternity case upon a showing of "service of process" on the defendant and any additional showing required by state law. In general, once the mother has identified a putative father, and the CSE agency is reasonably sure they have located his home or work address, the man must be notified that he has been named in a paternity case. This notification is typically a letter alleging his paternity and requesting his appearance at an appointment with the CSE agency or a court hearing, or submission to genetic testing. The putative father's receipt of this letter is called "service of process."[48]

Many observers have concerns about this provision of law because states and jurisdictions have broad discretion in determining what constitutes notice (i.e., service of process). Some jurisdictions consider publication notice, where a notice of the proceeding is put into the newspaper, as sufficient. Thus, even in situations in which some level of notice is required, federal law allows the mother, or the state in a welfare case, to obtain a

---

[46] University of Wisconsin - Madison, A Failed Relationship?, p. 12-17. See also: *Family Ties: Improving Paternity Establishment Practices and Procedures for Low-Income Mothers, Fathers and Children.* National Women's Law Center and Center on Fathers, Families, and Public Policy, p. 9-11.

[47] Anderson-Khleif, Susan. *Divorced But Not Disastrous: How to Improve the Ties Between Single Parent Mothers, Divorced Fathers, and the Children.* 1982. p. 148-150.

[48] U.S. Department of Health and Human Services. Office of the Inspector General. *Paternity Establishment – Administrative and Judicial Methods.* April 2000, OEI-06-98-00050. p. 5 [http://www.dhhs.gov/progorg/oei]

determination of paternity when the man named as the father is not present for the initial hearing or for subsequent paternity proceedings.

Some observers argue that the practice of using default judgments (i.e., judgments made in the absence of the alleged father) has adversely affected many putative fathers who claim they are not the father of the child in question but, for whatever reason, did not show up in court to deny the allegations.

Many observers maintain that the standards governing default judgments should balance the rights of the putative father to proper notice and the opportunity to be heard before paternity is established and a child support order set against the right of the child to obtain a determination of paternity and support (on a timely basis) from a father who knowingly fails to appear in court.[49]

When 95% Equals 100%

Federal law requires states to have procedures which create a rebuttable or, at the option of the state, conclusive presumption of paternity upon genetic testing results indicating a threshold probability that the alleged father is the actual father of the child. Most states have a rebuttable presumption paternity threshold that ranges from 95%-99.9%.

In some states, blood test results that indicate a 98% or greater probability of paternity are not rebuttable, which raises the possibility that 2% of the putative fathers tested may be wrongly assigned paternity, and thereby wrongly saddled with an 18-year financial responsibility.[50]

Where is the Money Going?

Some noncustodial fathers argue that they were hoodwinked into believing that if they voluntarily acknowledged paternity, any child support they paid would be helping their child. They contend that this is not so if the child's mother is receiving TANF benefits because instead of directly benefiting their children, their child support payments are used to pay the state back for welfare payments that the family is receiving.

---

[49] National Women's Law Center and the Center on Fathers, Families, and Public Policy. *Family Ties: Improving Paternity Establishment Practices and Procedures for Low-Income Mothers, Fathers, and Children.* November 2000. p. 21.

[50] University of Wisconsin - Madison. Institute for Research on Poverty. Paternity and Public Policy by Daniel R. Meyer. *Focus*, v. 14, no. 2, summer 1992.

The 1996 welfare reform law (P.L. 104-193) eliminated the mandatory $50 child support pass-through and disregard for TANF families; states are now allowed to set their own policies. As of February 2002, 26 states had chosen to eliminate the child support pass-through and disregard. In those states, none of the money paid by noncustodial parents on behalf of their children who are receiving TANF benefits goes to their children. All of it goes to the state and federal governments to reimburse welfare costs. This change in policy, together with the dramatic decrease in the TANF caseload, has significantly reduced the amount of child support that goes to children who receive cash welfare assistance. In FY1996, under the former AFDC program about $337 million in child support payments was passed through to AFDC families and disregarded in calculating the family's AFDC benefit. In FY2000, $165 million in child support payments was received by TANF families.

Once families leave the TANF rolls, they are entitled to receive all current support paid on their behalf. This was true under the former AFDC program as well. However, current law (as compared to former, pre-1996, law) allows former cash welfare families to receive a greater share of the child support arrearages collected on their behalf, by giving priority to their claims over the state's claim to arrearages assigned to it (in certain circumstances).[51]

Custodial parents also are dissatisfied with the current child support distribution system. Custodial parents are frustrated because they view child support arrearages as belonging to them. They argue that they had to rely on family and friends for financial assistance during periods when the noncustodial parent failed to pay child support that occurred before they went on welfare. They contend that they (and not the state) are entitled to any pre-welfare arrearage payments that are collected on their behalf. Advocates point out that while promising families priority in collecting arrearages owed to them as an inducement to encourage them to move off welfare as soon as possible, the states and the federal government keep for themselves collections made via the federal income tax refund offset program - the most lucrative form of arrearage collection. (In tax year 2000, $1.4 billion in overdue support was collected via U.S. claims on federal income tax refunds.)

---

[51] The exception occurs if the child support arrearages were collected by the state through the federal income tax offset program. In those cases, the state has priority over the former TANF family.

> Absent the restoration of the fundamental importance of both parents and sensitivity to preserving the child's emotional bonds and healthy contact with both parents, the future of children in our society will continue to portend disfunction and despair. Hope for substantial and beneficial improvement in the quality of life for our progeny lies in the changing of the American credo from "the flag, motherhood, and apple pie" to "the flag, motherhood, and fatherhood."
>
> **Source:** U.S. Commission on Interstate Child Support Minority Report. *Let the Fathers Return,* by Don Chavez. June 10, 1992. p.31.

Putative Father Registries

At the other end of the paternity establishment spectrum is the case of biological fathers who do not have the opportunity to assert their paternal rights. This can happen if the father is unaware of the pregnancy or loses contact with the mother. To protect the rights of biological fathers who want to assume parental rights and responsibilities, about half of the states have established paternity registries. Thus, in the event that the mother places the child up for adoption, the biological father will be notified of any proceedings to terminate his parental rights if he registers his claim to paternity. These paternity registries are viewed as a vehicle to limit the potential disruption to children and adoptive parents while protecting the rights of biological fathers.[52]

MOTHERS' RIGHTS AND CONCERNS

Historically one of the main reasons custodial mothers have cited for not having a child support award is that they did not pursue obtaining one. It is not known whether this is because they did not want any further contact with the child's father because of a belief that the child was better off without paternal contact, fear of domestic and/or sexual violence, an attitude that assumed that the man could not pay child support so why bother, or wanting to move on to another relationship without the complexity of the child's father always being in the picture.

---

[52] Center for Law and Social Policy. *Biology and Beyond: The Case for Passage of the New Uniform Parentage Act,* by Paula Roberts with assistance from Nicole Williams. October 2000. p. 30.

Women who are victims of domestic violence often face the conflict between the need for financial support from child support payments and the need for safety from abuse. Unless they choose to forego the child support payment because the risk of abuse is too great to warrant its pursuit, women who are victims of domestic violence must comply with the requirements for cooperation with the child support enforcement process. These requirements, however, can increase the risk of harm for the victim of domestic violence by bringing the victim and abuser into near proximity during courtroom proceedings; and/or angering an abuser by automatic procedures such as wage withholding or a driver's license suspension. However, if women who fear their abusers choose not to pursue child support, they impair their ability to become self-sufficient by relinquishing the child support resource for themselves and their children. Most victims of domestic violence do not want to forego these resources, and yet want to ensure their own safety and that of their children.[53] For the most part, women in these situations have to opt out of the CSE system through good cause exemptions or the 1996 welfare reform family violence option[54] and forego CSE services. Only a few states offer alternative case process services that help a custodial parent work out a safe plan for obtaining child support payments.[55]

BEST INTERESTS OF THE CHILD

Many observers maintain that the social, psychological, emotional, and financial benefits of having one's father legally identified are irrefutable. They suggest that paternity should be established, regardless of the ability of the father to pay child support. They argue that the role of both parents is critical in building the self-esteem of their children and helping the children become self-sufficient members of the community.

---

[53] Mathematica Policy Research Inc. *Making Child Support Safe: Coordinating Child Support and Public Assistance Agencies in Their Response to Domestic Violence,* by Ali Stieglitz and Amy Johnson. May 2001.

[54] The Family Violence Option (FVO) of the 1996 welfare law (P.L. 104-193) permits state TANF programs to waive federal rules regarding required work, time limited benefits, and child support cooperation for victims of domestic violence. The purpose of the FVO is to enable states to help victims of domestic violence without subjecting them to TANF rules that might "unfairly penalize" them or put them at further risk of abuse. Specifically, the FVO requires states that adopt it to: screen for and identify victims of domestic violence; refer victims of domestic violence to appropriate services; and grant "good cause" waivers to domestic violence victims when TANF requirements are harmful or unsafe. As of FY2000, 44 out of 54 jurisdictions with TANF programs had adopted the FVO.

[55] Center for Law and Social Policy. *Models for Safe Child Support Enforcement,* by Vicki Turetsky and Susan Notar. October 1999, p. 20.

Once paternity is established legally, a child gains legal rights and privileges. Among these may be rights to inheritance, rights to the father's medical and life insurance benefits, and to social security and possibly veterans' benefits. The child also has a chance to develop a relationship with the father, and to develop a sense of identity and connection to the "other half" of his or her family. It also may be important for the health of the child for doctors to have knowledge of the father's medical history.

It is often noted that legally establishing paternity is not the end of the story and that legally conferring fatherhood status on a man does not guarantee that the man will be a caring and responsible father. Some observers contend that a good relationship can exist without the formal establishment of legal paternity and a bad relationship cannot be fixed nor a previously nonexistent feeling created simply by establishing legal paternity. For some parents whose relationships are good, voluntarily establishing paternity can be an affirmation of their feelings for each other and the child. While for others parents with good relationships, who may be considering marriage to each other, paternity establishment may be viewed as a sign of distrust, and thereby inconsistent with eventual marriage. For some parents and communities, the father's informal acknowledgment – identifying the child as his to his family and friends and providing some financial support and help – may be more meaningful than a legal establishment of paternity. However, others note that if the relationship between the parents changes (e.g., becomes more adversarial), an informal acknowledgment may not provide as reliable a foundation for continuing support as a formal acknowledgment that legally establishes paternity.[56]

Moreover, some analysts argue that the child's perspective and concept of family and connectedness with both parents must be acknowledged and encouraged, regardless of whether his or her parents have separated, divorced, or never married. The strength of the emotional bonds within a family often greatly affect whether or not the child will become a good citizen and a responsible parent.

CONCLUDING REMARKS

Critics of the CSE program contend that even with an unprecedented array of "big brother" enforcement tools such as license (professional,

---

[56] National Women's Law Center and the Center on Fathers, Families, and Public Policy. *Family Ties: Improving Paternity Establishment Practices and Procedures for Low-Income Mothers, Fathers, and Children.* November 2000. p. 12.

driver's, recreational) and passport revocation; seizure of banking accounts, retirement funds, and lottery winnings; and automatic income withholding from pay checks, the program still collects only 17% of child support obligations for which it has responsibility and collects payments for only 42% of its caseload. Two reasons for the low rate of child support collections are (1) the low rate of paternity establishment; in FY2000 paternity was established for only 65% of the 10.1 million children in the CSE caseload who were born outside of marriage; and (2) many fathers cannot afford to pay; a study based on 1997 data indicated that 21% of noncustodial fathers were poor and thus had a limited ability to provide child support to their children.[57] A study based on 1999 data indicated that 30% of poor fathers and 72% of nonpoor fathers paid child support.[58]

In addition to increasing fathers' financial contributions, CSE policy may affect family formation behavior and how fathers relate to their children.[59] According to economic theory, stronger child support enforcement may increase the cost of children for men and should make men more reluctant to have children outside of marriage. In other words, by raising the cost of fatherhood to unmarried men, effective paternity establishment and child support enforcement deter non-marital births.[60] In contrast, stronger child support enforcement may reduce the cost of children for women (making them more willing to have children outside of marriage).[61] However, according to recent evidence, once a woman becomes a single mother, her chances of marrying anyone other than the father of her child are greatly reduced.[62]

It is also important to note that for children whose mothers and fathers both are poor, particularly children who receive TANF benefits, paternity establishment may not necessarily be economically beneficial. Because of child support distribution rules, child support paid on behalf of TANF families is retained by the state and the federal governments to reimburse

---

[57] The Urban Institute. Assessing the New Federalism, Discussion Papers. *A Look at Poor Dads Who Don't Pay Child Support,* by Elaine Sorensen and Chava Zibman. September 2000.
[58] The Urban Institute. *Policy Reforms are Needed to Increase Child Support from Poor Fathers,* by Elaine Sorensen and Helen Oliver. April 2002. p. 4.
[59] Center for Research on Child Wellbeing. Working Paper #01-13-FF, *Welfare Reform, Fertility and Father Involvement,* by Sara S. McLanahan and Marcia J. Carlson. January 8, 2002. p. 22.
[60] Center for Law and Social Policy. *The Importance of Child Support Enforcement: What Recent Social Science Research Tell Us,* by Paula Roberts. Spring 2002. p. 5.
[61] Joint Center for Policy Research. *The Impact of Child Support Enforcement on Nonmarital and Marital Births; Does it Differ by Racial and Age Groups?,* by Chien-Chung Huang. November 20, 2001. p. 5-6.
[62] Progressive Policy Institute. *Marriage as Public Policy,* by Daniel T. Lichter. Policy Report, September 2001.

them for cash welfare paid to the family. Nevertheless, this must be balanced by the tenet that in our society, parents are responsible for the financial well-being of their children and regardless of where their money actually goes, it is the duty of noncustodial parent to make child support payments.

Although the CSE program has historically been the policy answer to the problem of father absence, because its focus until recently was exclusively on financial support, it has had the practical effect of alienating many low-income fathers who are unable to meet their child support obligations. Many observers allege that the CSE program's focus on cost-recovery resulted in a CSE culture wherein noncustodial parents generally were viewed negatively, nonpaying noncustodial parents were viewed as lawbreakers, and putative fathers were seen as riffraff. It is generally agreed that the current policies and procedures pertaining to paternity establishment have made the process more efficient and non-combative, and that the technology exists to make the finding of paternity almost infallible. Some contend that the CSE program needs to change its perspective regarding putative fathers and send out a new message that highlights its service delivery mission, so that negative perceptions about the agency will not cause noncustodial parents and putative fathers to make inappropriate decisions.

Appendix A: Legislative History of Paternity Establishment Provisions

P.L. 90-248, the Social Security Amendments of 1967

This law required each state to establish a single organizational unit to establish paternity of children who were born out of wedlock and who were receiving AFDC.

P.L. 93-647, the Social Security Amendments of 1974

This law greatly increased federal intervention in state child support enforcement activities and created part D of Title IV of the Social Security Act. This new part, entitled "Child Support and Establishment of Paternity," required states, in order to receive AFDC funds, to operate a CSE program with specified components. Most of these had already been used in states that had been the most successful in implementing effective child support programs. Although the law left the basic responsibility for child support and establishment of paternity to the state, a far more active role was established for the federal government. P.L. 93-647 mandated more aggressive administration at both the federal and state levels, combined with financial incentives and penalties to encourage state compliance.

The primary responsibility for operating the CSE program was placed on the states pursuant to the state plan. A couple of the major requirements of a state plan were that: the state designate a single and separate organizational unit to administer the program and the state undertake to establish paternity and secure support for individuals receiving AFDC and others (i.e., non-AFDC families) who apply directly for CSE services. New eligibility requirements were added to the AFDC program requiring applicants for, or recipients of, AFDC to make an assignment of their child support rights to the state, to cooperate with the state in establishing paternity and securing support, and to furnish their Social Security number to the state.

P.L. 94-88, TARIFF AMENDMENTS, AMENDMENTS TO SOCIAL SECURITY ACT-1975

This law eased the requirement for AFDC recipients to cooperate with state CSE agencies when such cooperation would not be in the best interests of the child. (Good cause standards for refusing to cooperate in establishing paternity generally included situations that could result in physical or emotional harm to the child or caretaker relative, where legal procedures for adoption were underway, or where the child was conceived as a result of incest or rape.)

P.L. 98-378, THE CHILD SUPPORT ENFORCEMENT AMENDMENTS OF 1984

This law placed emphasis on improving both the child support enforcement and paternity establishment components of the program. It offered states incentives to make services available to both AFDC and non-AFDC families. It also required states to establish procedures that permitted the establishment of paternity any time prior to a child's 18th birthday.

In addition, the law permitted states to operate an approved child support research and demonstration project waiver under Section 1115 of the Social Security Act, provided certain conditions were met.

P.L. 100-485, THE FAMILY SUPPORT ACT OF 1988

This law required states to initiate the establishment of paternity for all children under the age of 18, including those for whom an action to establish paternity was previously dismissed because of the existence of a statute of limitations of less than 18 years. It encouraged states to create simple civil processes for voluntarily acknowledging paternity and civil procedures for establishing paternity in contested cases, and required states to have all parties in a contested paternity case take a genetic test upon the request of any party. It required the federal government to pay 90% of the laboratory costs of these tests, and permitted states to charge non-AFDC families for the cost of establishing paternity. It also set paternity establishment standards for the states. In addition, it required that each state, in administering any law involving the issuance of birth certificates, require both parents to furnish their Social Security Number (SSN), unless the state finds good cause for not doing so.

As noted above, states are required to meet federal standards for the establishment of paternity. The primary standard relates to the percentage obtained by dividing the number of children in the state who are born out of wedlock, are receiving cash benefits or CSE services, and for whom paternity has been established by the number of children who are born out of wedlock and are receiving cash benefits or CSE services. To meet federal requirements, this percentage in a state must: (1) be at least 50%; (2) be at least equal to the average for all states; or (3) have increased by 3 percentage points from fiscal years 1988 to 1991 and by 3 percentage points each year thereafter.

The 1988 law requires each state, in the administration of any law involving the issuance of a birth certificate, to require each parent to furnish his or her SSN, unless the state finds good cause for not requiring the parent to furnish it. The SSN must appear in the birth record but not on the birth certificate, and the use of the SSN obtained through the birth record is restricted to CSE purposes, except under certain circumstances. In addition, the law requires the HHS Secretary to maintain data, for both AFDC and non-AFDC families, on the number of cases needing and/or receiving CSE services, including paternity determination.

P.L. 103-66, THE OMNIBUS BUDGET RECONCILIATION ACT OF 1993

The 1993 reforms revised and added to the mandatory paternity establishment requirements imposed on states by the Family Support Act of 1988. The most notable provision increased the percentage of children, from 50% to 75% (i.e., paternity establishment percentage), for whom the state must establish paternity, which was backed up by financial penalties linked to a reduction of federal matching funds for the state's AFDC program. States were required to have in effect, by October 1, 1993, the following:

- A simple civil process for voluntarily acknowledging paternity under which the state must explain the rights and responsibilities of acknowledging paternity and afford due process safeguards. Procedures must include a hospital-based program for the voluntary acknowledgment of paternity during the period immediately preceding or following the birth of a child;

- A law under which the voluntary acknowledgment of paternity creates a rebuttable, or at state option, conclusive presumption of paternity, and under which such voluntary acknowledgments are admissible as evidence of paternity;

- A law under which the voluntary acknowledgment of paternity must be recognized as a basis for seeking a support order without requiring any further proceedings to establish paternity;

- Procedures which provide that any objection to genetic testing results must be made in writing within a specified number of days prior to any hearing at which such results may be introduced in evidence; if no objection is made, the test results must be admissible as evidence of paternity without the need for foundation testimony or other proof of authenticity or accuracy;

- A law which creates a rebuttable or, at the option of the state, conclusive presumption of paternity upon genetic testing results indicating a threshold probability of the alleged father being the father of the child;

- Procedures which require default orders in paternity cases upon a showing that process has been served on the defendant and whatever additional showing may be required by state law; and

- Expedited processes for paternity establishment in contested cases and full faith and credit to determinations of paternity made by other states.

P.L. 104-193, THE PERSONAL RESPONSIBILITY AND WORK OPPORTUNITY RECONCILIATION ACT OF 1996

The 1996 welfare reform law further strengthened the nation's paternity establishment system. In fact, many of the provisions adopted by PL. 103-66 were expanded and modified by P.L. 104-193. In addition to the basic requirement that voluntary acknowledgments must automatically become legal findings of parentage unless withdrawn, states are required: (1) to give full faith and credit to paternity affidavits signed in another state according to its procedures; (2) to bar judicial or administrative proceedings to ratify an unchallenged acknowledgment of paternity; and (3) to enter a default order in a paternity case upon a showing of service of process on the defendant and any additional showing required by state law.

P.L. 104-193 streamlined the paternity determination process; raised the paternity establishment requirement from 75% to 90%; implemented a simple civil process for establishing paternity; required a uniform affidavit to be completed by men voluntarily acknowledging paternity and entitled such affidavit to full faith and credit in any state; required both the mother and biological father to sign a voluntary acknowledgment of paternity and stipulated that a signed acknowledgment of paternity would be considered a legal finding of paternity unless rescinded within 60 days and thereafter may be challenged in court only on the basis of fraud, duress, or material mistake of fact; and provided that no judicial or administrative action is needed to ratify an acknowledgment that is not challenged. The 1996 law also required states to publicize the availability and encouraged the use of procedures for voluntary establishment of paternity and child support.

P.L. 105-33, THE BALANCED BUDGET ACT OF 1997

This law conformed the TANF penalty provisions to the CSE performance measures. It stipulated that the HHS Secretary may penalize states using graduated penalties that range between 1% and 5% of the TANF block grant amount and the penalties may be for failing to meet the paternity establishment percentages or other performance standards of the child support program or for either failing to submit required data or for submitting unreliable data to the Secretary. Before penalties are imposed, the state has a year to make corrective action. With regard to state laws providing expedited procedures, the 1997 law required that information pertaining to paternity or child support proceedings is to be filed with the state CSE case registry. The 1997 law allowed states, in voluntary paternity acknowledgment cases, to give the required notice of alternatives, legal consequences, and rights and responsibility through the use of video or audio equipment, rather than orally. Written notice is still required. The law also clarified that children excluded from the paternity establishment percentage calculation are excluded regardless of whether the state uses the CSE caseload as the base or all births in the state as a base.

INDEX

#

1996 welfare reform law, 26, 32

A

absent parents, 8
administrative processes, 7
adoption, 11, 44, 50
adultery, 40
Alabama, 3, 20, 27
Alaska, 3, 20
Arizona, 3, 20, 27
Arkansas, 3, 20
arrearages, 22, 41, 43

B

Balanced Budget Act, 54
Best Interests, 45
biological father(s), 1, 2, 9, 12, 13, 15, 39, 44, 53
biological parents, 13, 37
birth control, 38
Bush, President, 34

C

California, 3, 18, 19, 20, 38
cash benefits, 26, 51
cash support, 40
cash welfare, 28, 32, 34, 43, 48
Center on Fathers, 11, 33, 36, 41, 42, 46
Child Support Enforcement (CSE) vii,, ix, x, 1-5, 7, 10-12, 14, 15, 17, 18, 20-23, 25-28, 31-33, 35-37, 39, 41, 45-51, 54
child support order(s), 2, 5, 22
child support payments, 2, 22, 25, 41-43, 45, 48
child support, vii, ix, 1, 2, 7, 8, 11, 12, 13, 15, 17, 22, 25-28, 32-34, 36, 40, 42-45, 47-50, 53, 54
churches, 34
cohabiting families, 36
Colorado Child Support Improvement Project, 35
Colorado, 3, 20, 35
community organizations, 34
conception, 9
conclusive presumption, 14, 42, 52
conflict resolution, 8, 27
Connecticut, 3, 20

contested cases, 7, 9, 12, 51, 53
contested paternity, 11
cost-effectiveness, 22
court order, 8, 12
CSE agency(ies), x, 7, 8, 10, 11, 14, 26, 32, 33, 37, 41
CSE law, 9, 17
CSE program, x, 8, 18, 21, 25, 31, 33, 39, 41, 48
custodial mothers, 44
custodial parent, 26, 45
custody, 11, 13, 36

D

dead-beat dads, vii
default judgments, 41, 42
default order, 41, 53
Delaware, ix, 2, 3, 20
deoxyribonucleic acid (DNA), vii, ix, 12-15, 36
determining paternity, 7, 14
disciplinarian, 32, 40
District of Columbia, 3, 18, 20
divorced parents, 1, 25
DNA tests, ix, 13
domestic violence, 32, 33, 45
due process, 9, 33, 35, 40, 52
duress, 18, 53

E

economic support, 1
egg donors, x, 39
enforcement tools, 2, 46
exclusion testing, 13

F

family formation, 28, 47
Family Support Act, 51, 52
Fatherhood Grant Programs, 28, 34
fatherhood programs, 25, 27, 28, 34

federal government, 4, 14, 26, 28, 43, 49, 51
federal income tax refund offset program, 43
federal law, 14, 22, 25, 26, 35, 41, 42
federal matching rate, 5, 14
federal requirements, 19, 23, 51
federal standards, 10, 18, 21, 51
financial assistance, 43
financial benefits, 1, 45
financial penalties, 2, 52
financial responsibility, 38, 42
financial support, 2, 32, 45, 46, 48
Florida, 3, 20, 27
food stamp, 26, 35
foster care, 26
fraud, 18, 53

G

gender, 3, 33
genetic test(s)ing, vii, x, 5, 7-9, 12, 14, 15, 18, 26, 37, 39, 41, 42, 52
Georgia, 3, 20, 27
grandparents, 11
Guam, 3, 18, 20

H

Hawaii, 3, 20
Health and Human Services (HHS), 2, 4, 7, 8, 12, 15, 21-23, 25, 27, 32, 34, 35, 41, 51, 54
healthy marriages, 34
HHS Inspector General, 7, 8, 15
hospital-based paternity acknowledgment procedures, 35
hospital-based programs, x, 9, 32, 36
human leukocyte antigen (HLA), 12-14

I

Idaho, 3, 20

Illinois, 3, 20, 38
immigration status, 11
Incentive Funding Work Group, 23
incentive payment system, 22, 23
incentive system, 22, 23
income sources, 10
Indiana, 3, 20, 27, 38
inheritance, 17, 46
Institute for Responsible Fatherhood and Family Revitalization, 27
insurance benefits, 46
Iowa, 3, 20

J

job advancement skills, 27
job training, 27

K

Kansas, ix, 2, 3, 20
Kentucky, 3, 20

L

law enforcement, 11
legal father, 1, 15
legal paternity, 46
legal proceedings, 11, 26
legally identified father, 1, 18
litigation, 15
living expenses, 41
Louisiana, 3, 20
low-income fathers, 32, 34, 40, 48

M

Maine, 3, 20
Maintenance-of-Effort (MOE), 28
married couple(s), x, 8, 9
married fatherhood, 34
married-couple families, 25, 28
Maryland, 3, 20, 27, 38
Massachusetts, 3, 20

media campaigns, x, 27, 32, 34, 37
mediation services, 27
Medicaid, 1, 26
Michigan, 3, 21, 38
Minnesota, 4, 21, 27
Mississippi, 4, 21, 27
Missouri, 4, 21, 27
Montana, 4, 20, 21
Mothers' Rights, 44
multiple filing agencies, 10

N

National Fatherhood Initiative, 27
National Women's Law Center, 11, 33, 36, 41, 42, 46
Nebraska, 4, 21
Nevada, 4, 21
never-married, 1, 25
New Hampshire, 4, 21
New Jersey, 4, 21, 38
New Mexico, 4, 20, 21
New York, iii, iv, 21
newborns, 14, 31, 37
noncash aid, 40
noncooperation, 26
noncustodial parent(s), ix, 2, 10, 12, 17, 25, 27, 33, 40, 43, 48
nonmarital births, ix, 2
North Carolina, 4, 21, 27
North Dakota, 4, 21

O

Office of Child Support Enforcement (OCSE), ix, 1, 4, 12, 15, 21, 25, 35
Ohio, 4, 21, 38
Oklahoma, 4, 21
older children, x, 31, 32, 37
Omnibus Budget Reconciliation Act, 35, 52
Oregon, 4, 21
outreach campaigns, 37

P

parental liability, 2
parenting education, 27
past-due child support, 22
paternal rights, 44
paternity acknowledgment affidavit, 9
paternity affidavits, 35, 53
paternity concerns, x, 39
paternity determination, 31, 51, 53
paternity establishment percentage, 18-20, 23, 52, 54
paternity establishment process, x, 5, 8, 32, 36, 40
paternity registries, 44
paternity tests(ing), 12, 13
peer support, 27
penalty for noncompliance, 21
penalty, 22, 23, 26, 54
Pennsylvania, 4, 21, 27
Personal Responsibility and Work Opportunity Reconciliation Act, 22, 53
personal responsibility, 2, 27, 34
policy options, vii, x, 5
poverty, 2
presumptive paternity, 8
prison systems, 34
public policy, ix, 2
public service announcements, 37
public welfare, ix, 17
publication notice, 41
Puerto Rico, ix, 2, 4, 18, 21
putative fathers, ix, 10, 13-15, 37, 39, 42, 48

R

race, 33
red blood cell antigen testing, 12
red cell enzyme and serum protein electrophoresis, 12
Rhode Island, 4, 21

S

self-sufficient, 28, 45
separated, 25, 46
service of process, 41, 53
single mothers, 2
single-parent families, vii, ix, 2, 27, 34
Social Security Act, 10, 17, 18, 25, 26, 49, 50
Social Security Number (SSN), 9, 32, 50, 51
Social Services Block Grant, 28
South Carolina, 4, 21, 38
South Dakota, 4, 21
sperm donors, x, 39
State and National New Hires Directories, 37
statutory rape, 11
support payments, 22, 26, 43
surrogate mothers, x, 39

T

TANF block grant, 25, 26, 28, 54
Tariff Amendments, 50
Temporary Assistance to Needy Families (TANF), ix, x, 1, 5, 11, 18, 22, 25, 26, 28, 32, 33, 35, 42, 43, 45, 47, 54
Tennessee, 4, 21, 27
Texas, 4, 21
threshold probability, 14, 42, 52
two-parent families, 25, 28

U

unmarried parents, 10, 12, 37
unmarried women, ix, 1, 2
Utah, 4, 21

V

Vermont, 4, 21

Virgin Islands, 4, 18, 21
Virginia, 4, 21, 27
visitation, 11, 25, 27, 28, 36, 41
voluntary acknowledgment, ix, 7-10, 31, 35, 36, 52, 53

W

wages garnished, 41
welfare assistance, 9, 35, 43
welfare families, ix, 18, 43
welfare fraud, 11

welfare payments, 42
welfare reform law, 10, 12, 27, 43, 53
welfare reform, 10, 12, 27, 43, 45, 53
welfare-to-work, 28
Wisconsin, 4, 21, 27, 33, 41, 42
work programs, 34
Wyoming, 4, 21

Y

year of birth, 18, 20